A Brief History of Panics in the United States

A Brief History of Panics in the United States

CLEMENT JUGLAR;
DECOURCEY W. THOM, ED.

NEW YORK

A Brief History of Panics in the United States
Cover © 2006 Cosimo, Inc.

For information, address:

Cosimo, P.O. Box 416
Old Chelsea Station
New York, NY 10113-0416

or visit our website at:
www.cosimobooks.com

A Brief History of Panics in the United States was
originally published in 1916.

Cover design by www.kerndesign.net

ISBN: 1-59605-487-5

A Crisis or Panic may be defined as a stoppage or the rise of prices: that is to say, the period when new buyers are not to be found. It is always accompanied by a reactionary movement in prices. A panic may be broadly stated as due to overtrading...
—from the Introduction

INTRODUCTION

COMPRISING A CONDENSATION OF THE THEORY
OF PANICS, BY M. JUGLAR, RENDERED INTO
ENGLISH, WITH CERTAIN ADDITIONAL MA-
TERIAL, BY DeCOURCEY W. THOM.

IN this translation, made with the
author's consent, my chief object being to
convey his entire meaning, I have unhesi-
tatingly rendered the French very freely
sometimes, and again very literally. Style
has thus suffered for the sake of clear-
ness and brevity, necessary to secure
and retain the attention of readers of this
class of books. This same conciseness has
also been imposed on our author by the in-
herent dryness and minuteness of his faith-
ful inquiry into hundreds of figures, tables
showing the condition of banks at the time
of various panics, etc., etc., essential to his
demonstration. As an extreme instance of
the latitude I have sometimes allowed my-

self, I cite my rendering of the title: "*Des Crises Commerciales et de Leur Retour Periodique en France, en Angleterre et aux États-Unis*" merely as "Panics and Their Periodical Occurrence in the United States": for M. Juglar himself states that a commercial panic is always a financial panic, as a falling away of the metallic reserve indicates its breaking out; and I have only translated that portion dealing with the United States, deeming the rest unnecessary, for this amply illustrates and proves the theorem in hand.

To this sketch of the financial history of the United States up to 1889, when M. Juglar published his second edition, I have added a brief account to date, including the panic of 1890, the table headed "National Banks of the United States," and some additions to the other tables scattered through this book.

From the prefaces to the French editions of 1860 and of 1889, and other introductory matter, I have condensed his theory as follows:

A Crisis or Panic may be defined as a

stoppage ot the rise of prices: that is to say, the period when new buyers are not to be found. It is always accompanied by a reactionary movement in prices.

A panic may be broadly stated as due to overtrading, which causes general business to need more than the available capital, thus producing general lack of credit. Its precipitating causes are broadly anything leading to overtrading:

In the United States they may be classed as follows:

1. **Panics of Circulation,** as in 1857, when the steadily increased circulation, which had almost doubled in nine years, had rendered it very easy to grant excessive discounts and loans, which had thus overstimulated business so that the above relapse occurred; or, we may imagine the converse case, leading to a quicker and even greater disaster: a sudden and proportionate shrinkage of circulation, which, of course, would have fatally cut down loans and discounts, and so precipitated general ruin.

2. A Panic of Credit, as in 1866, when the failure of Overend, Gurney, & Co. rendered the whole business world over cautious, and led to a universal shrinkage of credit. [I take the liberty of adding that it seems evident to me that such a danger must soon confront us in the United States, unless our Silver Law is changed, because of a finally inevitable distrust of the government's ability to keep 67-cent silver dollars on an equality with 100-cent gold dollars.]

3. Panics of Capital, as in 1847, when capital was so locked up in internal improvements as to prove largely useless.

4. General Tariff Changes. To the three causes given above the translator adds a fourth and most important one: Any change in our tariff laws general enough to rise to the dignity of a new tariff has with one exception in our history precipitated a panic. This exception is the tariff of 1846, which was for revenue only, and introduced after long notice and upon a graduated scale. This had put the nation at large in such good condition that when the apparently inevitable Decennial Panic occurred in 1848 recovery from it was very speedy.

The reason for this general effect of new tariffs is obvious. Usual prices and confidence are so disturbed that buyers either hold off, keeping their money available, or else draw unusually large amounts so as to buy stock before adverse tariff changes, thus tightening money in both ways by interfering with its accustomed circulation. This tendency towards contraction spreads and induces further withdrawal of deposits, thus requiring the banks to reduce their loans ; and so runs on and on to increasing discomfort and uneasiness until panic is speedily produced. The practical coincidence and significance of our tariff changes and panics is shown by an extract below from an article written by the translator in October–November, 1890, predicting the recent panic which was hastened somewhat by the Baring collapse.[1]

---

[1] *Inter-relations of Tariffs, Panics, and the Condition of Agriculture, as Developed in the History of the United States of America.*

This brief sketch of our economic history in the United States seeks to show that Protective Tariffs have always im-

The retarding or precipitating influence of a good or bad condition of agriculture upon the advent of a panic is also indicated.

poverished a majority of our people, the Agriculturists ; that agriculture has thus been made a most unprofitable vocation throughout the States, and that this unsoundness at the very foundation of the business of the American people has often forced our finances into such makeshift conditions, that under any unusual financial strain a panic, with all its wretched accompaniments, has resulted.

To consider this properly, we must note the well known fact that in this land, those who live by agriculture directly, are more than one half of our population. Their votes can cause to be made such laws as they see fit, hence, one would expect the enactment of laws to raise the price of farm products, and to lower the price of all that the farmer has to buy. But the farmers vote as the manufacturers and other active classes of the minority of our voters may influence ; and only twice in our history, from 1789 to 1808, and from 1846 to 1860, have enough of the minority found their interests sufficiently identical with that of the unorganized farmer-majority to join votes, and thus secure at once their common end. In consequence of this coalition during these two periods, two remarkable things happened : 1st, agriculture flourished, and comfortable living was more widely spread : 2d, panics were very infrequent, and the hardships and far-reaching discomforts that must ever attend adjustments to new financial conditions after disturbances were, of course, minimized.

It is not fair to deduce very much from the first period of prosperity among the farmers, 1789 to 1808, for, during this time, there were no important business interests unconnected with agriculture ; but we may summarize the facts that from 1789 to 1808, there was, 1st, no protection, the average duty during this time being 5 per cent., and that laid for revenue only ; 2d, that agriculture flourished ; 3d, that there was not a single panic.

The symptoms of approaching panic, generally patent to every one, are wonderful prosperity as indicated by very numer-

---

" The Embargo " of 1808, followed by the Non-Intercourse Act in 1809 and the War of 1812-15, and the war tariff, by which double duties were charged in order to raise money for war purposes, caused us to suffer all the economic disasters flowing from tariffs ranging between absolute protection, and those practically prohibiting, and intensified by the sufferings inseparable from war.

During this period agriculture, for the first time in our history, was in a miserable condition. It is significant that for the first time too, we had a protective tariff. Though our people made heroic efforts to make for themselves those articles formerly imported, thus starting our manufacturing interests, they had, of course, lost their export trade and its profits. When the peace of 1814 came, we again began exporting our produce, and aided by the short harvests abroad, and our own accumulated crops, resumed the profitable business which for six years our farmers and our people generally had entirely lost.

Our first panic, that of 1814, came as a result of our long exclusion from foreign markets, being followed by the stimulation given business through resumption of our foreign trade in 1814, which was immensely heightened by the banks issuing enormous quantities of irredeemable paper, instead of bending all their energies to paying off the paper they had issued during the war.

But worse than the suffering entailed by this panic, was the engrafting upon our economic policy of the fallacious theory made possible by the Embargo and the Non-Intercourse Act, (which was equivalent, let me enforce it once more, to that highest protective tariff, a prohibitory one) that *all infant manufactures must be protected, that is, guaranteed a home market*, though such home market be one where all goods cost more to the purchaser than similar goods bought elsewhere,

ous enterprises and schemes of all sorts,
by a rise in the price of all commodities,
of land, of houses, etc., etc., by an active

and this in order that the compact little band of sellers in the
home market may make their profit.   This demand for protection was made by those who had started manufactures during the years from 1808 to the end of the war of 1815, when,
as we have seen, imports were practically excluded.

In 1816 their demand met explicit assent, for, in the tariff of
that year, duty for protection, not for revenue, was granted ;
and an average of 25 per cent. duties for six years, to be followed by an average of 20 per cent. duties, was laid upon
imports.   For a few years bad bread crops in Europe, demand
for our cotton, and an inflation of our currency delayed a
panic.

But, we had started on our unreasoning course.   We had
tried to ignore the laws of demand and supply, and had for-
gotten that it is also artificial to attempt preventing purchases
in the cheapest, and selling in the highest markets ; and to
help a few manufacturers we had put up prices for all that a
large majority of our population,—the agriculturists mainly—
had to buy.   In a short while the demand for what the
farmers had to sell fell away, and bills could not be met, and
their troubles were added to those of the minority of the con-
sumers of the country ; the volume of business fell off, and a
panic came in 1818.   The influences that led up to it continued until 1846, as follows :   The great factors in producing
this state of affairs were the successive tariffs of 1818, with
its 25 per cent. duty upon cottons and woollens, and its increased duties on all forms of manufactured iron, (the tariff of
1824 which increased duties considerably), and the tariff of
1828, imposing an average of 50 per cent. duties, and in which
the protective movement reached its acme (omitting, of course,
the present McKinley Bill with its 60 per cent. average duty).
In 1832, consequently, a great reaction in sentiment took

request for workmen, a rise in salaries, a lowering of interest, by the gullibility of the public, by a general taste for speculating in order to grow rich at once, by a growing luxury leading to excessive expenditures, a very large amount of discounts and loans and bank notes[1] and a very small

---

place, and the " Compromise Tariff " was passed and duties were lowered. From this period, the advocacy of a high tariff in order to protect " Infant Industries," no longer "Infant" was largely abandoned, and its advocacy was generally based upon the fallacy, less obvious then than now, of securing high wages to laborers by means of high import duties. This plea for high duties the laborer found to be fallacious.

They (agriculturists mainly) found that they had to pay more for manufactured goods, so that the manufacturers could still buy their raw materials at the advanced prices, pay themselves the accustomed or increased profits, and then possibly pay the laborer a small advance in wages.

The advance did not compensate for increased cost of necessaries of life. If competition reduced the manufacturers' profit, the first reduction of expenses was always in the laborer's pay. The recognition of these truths brought about the further reduction of duties until 1842, in which year the tariff was once more raised. It was not until 1846 that we enjoyed a tariff which sought to eliminate the protective features. It is significant that a period of greater profit and stability among our business men, but especially among our

---

[1] Our recent banking history has proved rather an exception to this law as far as bank notes are concerned, because of the obviously unusual cause of sudden and enormous calling in of government bonds, the basis of bank-note issue.

reserve in specie and legal-tender notes and
poor and decreasing deposits.

On the other hand, the lowest point of

---

farmers, was then inaugurated.   This was the first tariff, since
that of 1816, not affected by politics.   It lasted until 1857,
and the country flourished marvellously under it.

From 1816, when protection was first resorted to, until to-
day, tariff rates have been almost continually raised, mainly
by votes of the agriculturists, misled by the manufacturers and
politicians, influenced by the manufacturers' money.   And a
fact worth noting is that financial panics have come quick
and furious.   They came in 1818, and in 1825–26, in 1829–30,
and so on, (see page 13).   Sudden changes in our tariff rates
have unvaryingly been followed by financial panics within a
short period.   Changes to lower rates have not brought panics
so quickly as changes in the reverse direction.

Low tariff without protective features, maintained steadily,
has been coincident with constantly increasing prosperity to
the country at large : but most especially to the agriculturists.
This is readily understood, for purchases of imported and manufactured goods and all outfit needed for the farmers' land
and family can be made at low—and owing to the competition
that always arises to supply a steady and natural market—lowering prices.   Moreover, the settled prices prevailing throughout the country allow of assured calculations and precautions
as to business ventures, and permit such a ratio to be established between expenses and income, that at the end of the
fiscal year a profit, not a loss, may be counted upon.

This was the experience of our agriculturists during the
second and last prosperous time of our farmers, 1846–60.
During that period agriculture flourished ; the tariff was low
and there were only two panics, that of 1848, and the one of
1857, and the first (a non-protective one) should not be considered as precipitated by the tariff of 1846, except that some
few suffered briefly in readjusting themselves to the changed,

depression following a panic is accompanied by the converse of the symptoms just enumerated.

(though better),condition of the new tariff. The vast majority of the nation reaped enormous benefits from the changes inaugurated.

The panic of 1857 was caused by over-activity in trade speculation, and over-banking, and the tariff of the same year was really passed to help avert the panic threatening. It had the contrary effect, it is believed, for it still further, of course, unsettled rates for goods, when prices were already unstable. But the point is to be noted that in reality tariff change followed practical panic in this instance rather than practical panic tariff change. The high protective war tariffs, beginning in 1860, and increased for war purposes and granted largely as an offset for those internal revenue taxes laid to carry on the war, have been continued as a body ever since, as is well known, despite the internal revenue taxes having been abolished except on whiskey and tobacco. It is equally well known that farming has grown less and less remunerative since 1860, and that the panics of 1864, 1873, and 1884 have been unfortunate culminations of almost unceasing financial discomfort, which has been most forcibly exemplified during the last two months. Even now the financial fabric is in unstable equilibrium, and this latest monstrosity—the McKinley Bill—imposing the highest tariff we have ever exacted—an average duty of 60 per cent., and coming when a panic was due, bids fair to hurry us into another and a terrible financial panic. If it does not do so, it will be because our crops are too bountiful to allow it, but it will at least have made the agriculturists and all buyers of other commodities than agricultural produce pay more for all purchases. It will bring no more money into their pockets, but it must take out considerably more. The people appreciate this. The nation's pocket nerve has been touched. This is the meaning

Bank balance sheets reflect in cold figures the result of the above influences. Prices being high, and discounts and loans

of the recent election, it seems to the writer. But whether the impending danger can be averted even if a prompt, though wise and slow reversal of tariff policy can be forced by the next Congress is doubtful, for unrest and timidity have been evoked and require time to be allayed before easy and orderly business operations will in general be resumed, unless indeed bountiful crops here and demand abroad once again reverse the logic of the situation.

Certain it is that our tariff laws must interfere as little as possible with the natural law of demand and supply in making prices, or we must be content to suffer from the instability that artificiality always brings with it.

Our plain duty is to enact as speedily as possible a tariff that shall by small but continued changes cut down our protective duties and substitute non-protective duties until our tariff is for revenue only ; for thus and thus only can the vast majority of the agriculturists buy what they need most cheaply, and so find that to purchase necessaries does not cost them more than the total of their sales ; and our exports of produce, chiefly owing to agricultural prosperity, would increase, thus materially helping to build up our general business so that the other nations will have to pay us, in the gold we require for comfortable management of our business, the growing trade balances against them.

The rough table below suggests that sudden tariff changes have precipitated panics, which have come quickly if the change was to higher protective duties and somewhat slower if the change was to lower protective duties ; that slow and well considered changes doing away with protective duties generally have not caused disturbances ; and that agriculture has flourished in proportion as we approached tariff for revenue only. It has for obvious reasons required about one year for

large in proportion to deposits, and having steadily increased for years, danger
is near ; further, when discounts and loans

---

financial trouble to be shown by decrease in value of farm
produce as evinced by wheat-flour exports.

Special conditions, such as excessive wheat corps here and
deficiency abroad or special tariff favors to flour export, may
even increase the amount exported despite an otherwise untoward effect of the new tariff upon farmers. I have selected
flour exports as the article best reflecting the chief interest of
the farmers, and at the same time the state of general business
for manufacturing, transportation and such other branches as
are concerned with it.

TARIFFS.	They have all been designedly Protective save the one of 1846.	Panics.	Condition of agriculture and incidentally of general business as suggested by export of wheat-flour from 1790–1890.		
			Year.	Barrels.	Dollars.
			1790..	724,623	4,591,293
			1791..	619,681	3,408,246
			1792..	824,464	....
			1793..1,074,639		....
			1794..	846,010	....
			1795..	687,369	....
			1796..	725,194	....
			1797..	515,633	....
			1798..	567,558	....
			1799..	519,265	....
			1800..	653,056	....
			1801..1,102,444		....
			1802..1,156,248		....
			1803..1,311,853		9,310,000
			1804..	810,008	7,100,000
			1805..	777,513	8,325,000
			1806..	782,724	6,867,000

Introduction.

are not only large in proportion to deposits, having increased steadily for years, and then suddenly fallen off noticeably for a

		1807..1,249,819	10,753,000
		1808.. 263,813	1,936,000
		1809.. 846,247	5,944,000
		1810.. 798,431	6,846,000
		1811..1,445,012	14,662,000
Say 1814 { Practical exclusion of all imports through the war = Prohibitory Tariff. }	1814	1812..1,443,492	13,687,000
		1813..1,260,943	13,591,000
		1814.. 193,274	1,734,000
		1815.. 862,739	7,209,000
1816 { Duties for six years @ 25% and thereafter @ 20%. }		1816.. 729,053	7,712,000
		1817..1,479,198	17,751,376
	1818	1818..1,157,697	11,576,970
		1819.. 750,669	6,005,280
		1820..1,177,036	5,296,664
1818 { Duties 25% on Cotton and Woollens, and all duties on Manufactured Iron increased. }		1821..1,056,119	4,298,043
		1822.. 827,865	5,103,280
		1823.. 756,702	4,962,373
		1824.. 996,792	5,759,176
	1825–26	1825.. 813,906	4,212,127
		1826.. 857,820	4,121,466
		1827.. 868,492	4,420,081
		1828.. 860,809	4,286,939
		1829.. 837,385	5,793,651
1828 { Average duty of 50%. }		1830..1,227,434	6,085,953
		1831..1,806,529	9,938,458
		1832.. 864,919	4,880,623
		1833.. 955,768	5,613,010
		1834.. 835,352	4,520,781
		1835.. 779,396	4,394,777
		1836.. 505,400	3,572,599
1833 { Compromise Tariff, gradual reduction of duties from 50% average until In 1842 the average was 20%. But this was levied for Protection not merely for Revenue. }	1836–39	1837.. 318,719	2,987,269
		1838.. 448,161	3,603,299
		1839.. 923,151	6,925,170
		1840..1,897,501	10,143,615
		1841..1,515,817	7,759,646
		1842..1,283,602	7,375,356
1842 { Imposed higher duties. }		1843.. 841,474	3,763,073
		1844..1,438,574	6,759,488
		1845..1,195,230	5,398,593

considerable time, only to increase again, danger is imminent.

On the other hand, a steady and radical

1846 { Imposed lower duties and these were not for Protection purposes they were simply for Revenue. }	1848	1846..2,289,476 11,668,669
		1847..4,382,496 26,133,811
		1848..2,119,393 13,194,109
		1849..2,108,013 11,280,582
		1850..1,385,448 7,098,570
		1851..2,202,335 10,524,331
		1852..2,799,339 11,869,143
		1853..2,920,918 14,783,394
		1854..4,022,386 27,701,444
		1855..1,204,540 10,896,908
		1856..3,510.626 29,275,148
1857 { Reduced Tariff rates on above plan because of redundant prosperity. }	1857	1857..3,712,053 25,882,316
		1858..3,512,169 19,328,884
		1859..2,431,824 14,433,591
1860 { War Tariff protection restored as compensation for Internal Revenue taxes. }	1864	1860..2,611,596 15,448,507
		1861..4,323,756 24,645,849
1862..As above..........		1862..4,882,033 27,534,677
1864..As above..........		1863..4,390,055 28,366,069
		1864..3,557,347 25,588,249
		1865..2,641,298 27,507,084
		1866..2,183,050 18,396,686
		1867..1,300,106 12,803,775
		1868..2,076,423 20,887,798
		1869..2,431,873 18,813,865
		1870..3,463,333 21,169,593
		1871..3,653,841 24,093,184
1872 { 10% reduction, but coffee and tea put on Free List and whiskey and tobacco taxes reduced. }	1873	1872..2,514,535 17,955,684
		1873..2,562,086 19,381,664
		1874..4,094,094 29,258,094
		1875..3,973,128 23,712,440
		1876..3,935,512 24,433,470
1875 { 10% reduction above repealed. }		1877..3,343,665 21,663,947
		1878..3,947,333 25,095,721
		1879..5,629,714 29,567,713
		1880..6,011,419 35,333,197
		1881..7,945,786 45,047,257
		1882..5,915,686 36,375,055

reduction of loans and discounts, following
a panic and extending until new enterprises are very scarce, till prices are very
low, till there is wide-spread idleness
among workmen, a decrease in salaries and
in interest rates, when the public is wary
and speculation dead, and expenditures
are cut down as far as possible, may be
taken to mean a rapid and continued resumption of every prosperous business : but
if the above process is only partially performed, renewed trouble must result;—in
other words, liquidation to really be helpful
(to congested business) must be thorough.

A study of the first of the following
tables, " National Banks of the United
States," illustrates the above generaliza-
tion. It is unnecessary to mention that
1873, 1884, and 1890 have been the

1883 { Duties really raised on class of goods most used, but apparently lowered the tariff, for it considerably reduced rates on many little used classes of goods.	1884	1883..9,205,664	54,824,459
		1884..9,152,260	51,139,695
		1885.10,648,145	52,146,336
		1886..8,179,241	38,442,955
		1887.11,518,449	51,950,082
		1888.11,963,574	54,777,710
		1889..9,374,803	45,296,485
1890 { McKinley Bill average of 60% duty.	1890	1890.12,231,711	57,036,168
		1891.11,344,304	54,705,616

		1892..15,196,769	75,362,283
1893-4	Free silver and sudden ill-distributed and drastic tariff reductions and insufficient revenue.	1893..16,620,339	75,494,347
		1894..16,859,533	69,271,770
		1895..15,268,892	51,651,928
		1896..14,620,864	52,025,217
1897		1897..14,569,545	55,914,347
		1898..15,349,943	69,263,718
		1899..18,485,690	73,093,870
		1900..18,699,194	67,760,886
		1901..18,650,979	69,459,296
		1902..17,759,203	65,661,974
1903	Tariff disturbance to higher rates. The propaganda for keener regulation of business.	1903..19,716,484	73,756,404
		1904..16,699,432	68,894,836
		1905.. 8,826,335	40,176,136
		1906..13,919,048	59,106,869
1907		1907..15,584,667	62,175,397
		1908..13,937,247	64,170,508
		1909..10,521,161	51,157,366
		1910.. 9,040,987	47,621,467
		1911..10,129,435	49,386,946
		1912..11,006,487	50,999,797
1913	Tariff reductions to produce a revenue; not on a protective basis. The further regulating of business. The "World War."	1913..11,394,805	53,171,537
		1914..12,768,073	62,391,503

TABLE NO. 1.—NATIONAL BANKS OF THE UNITED STATES.

YEAR	MONTH	LOANS AND DISCOUNTS. Millions	"WORKING CAPITAL." In Millions — Capital.	"WORKING CAPITAL." — Undivided Profits and Surplus, etc.	"WORKING CAPITAL." — Deposits.	"WORKING CAPITAL." — TOTAL. Millions	Excess of Capital (Surplus, Undivided Profits, plus Deposits) over Loans and Discounts. Millions	Percentage "Working Capital" exceeds Loans and Discounts.	Difference between Deposits and Loans and Discounts. Millions	Percentage of Difference (over or under) between Deposits and Loans and Discounts.
1863	Oct. 5	186	135	20	183	338	152	65.4	+ 17	35.4 over
1864	Jany. 4	500	403	71	522	996	496	69.2	+ 22	45.4 "
1865	Jany. 2	608	420	86	558	1064	456	47.7	− 50	9.2 "
1866	Jany. 1	616	420	101	534	1055	439	49.8	− 82	9.9 "
1867	Jany. 7	644	419	116	568	1103	459	42.8	− 76	4.8 under
1868	Jany. 6	688	426	124	546	1096	408	41.6	− 142	15.3 "
1869	Jany. 4	767	444	140	561	1145	378	46.4	− 206	13.3 "
1870	Jany. 22	839	464	147	593	1204	365	37.2	− 257	26.7 "
1871	Mch. 18	913	484	163	656	1303	390	33.	− 246	36.7 "
1872	Feby. 27	897	490	173	595	1258	361	30.3	− 302	41.4 "
*1873	Feby. 28	956	496	182	647	1325	369	29.9	− 309	29.1 "
1874	Feby. 27	950	504	184	620	1308	358	28.6	− 330	52.4 "
1875	Mch. 1	920	493	167	659	1319	399	27.8	− 261	47. "
1876	Mch. 10	854	473	165	602	1240	386	27.3	− 252	53.8 "
1877	Jany. 20	823	462	153	643	1258	435	30.2	− 180	39.6 "
1878	Mch. 15	774	454	159	648	1261	487	31.1	− 126	41.9 "
1879	Jany. 1	773	458	176	633	1267	494	34.5	− 146	27.9 "
1880	Feby. 21	1182	469	191	1036	1696	514	33.3	− 140	14.9 "
1881	Mch. 11	1249	490	196	1004	1690	441	31.5	− 245	15. "
1882	Mch. 11	1321	515	209	1046	1770	449	30.3	− 275	14. "
1883	Mch. 13	1232	524	206	996	1726	494	26.1	− 236	24.5 "
*1884	Mch. 7	1367	533	212	1152	1897	530	25.3	− 215	26.8 "
1885	Mch. 10	1515	555	231	1224	2010	495	28.6	− 291	20.6 "
1886	Mch. 10	1584	582	246	1251	2079	495	27.9	− 237	18.0 "
1887	Mch. 4	1704	596	269	1354	2219	515	24.6	− 333	23.7 "
1888	Feby. 14	1844	626	290	1479	2395	551	23.7	− 350	26.8 "
1889	Feby. 26	1927	662	316	1483	2461	534	23.1	− 365	25.8 "
*1890	Feby. 28	2044	679	330	1702	2711	667	22.2	− 444	24.0 "
1891	Feby. 26							21.7	− 342	29.2 "
1892	Mch. 1							24.6		20.1 "

Note.—These figures are for the standing at the first part of the year as indicated.

* Panic Years.

TABLE NO. 1.—NATIONAL BANKS OF THE UNITED STATES.—Continued.

YEAR	MONTH	LOANS AND DISCOUNTS. (Millions)	"WORKING CAPITAL." (In Millions.)				Excess of Capital (Surplus, Undivided Profits, and Deposits) over Loans and Discounts. (Millions)	Percentage "Working Capital" exceeds Loans and Discounts.	Difference between Deposits and Loans and Discounts. (Millions)	Percentage of Difference (over or under) between Deposits and Loans and Discounts.
			Capital.	Undivided Profits and Surplus, etc.	Deposits.	TOTAL.				
1893	Mch. 6	2159	688	348	1751	2787	627	22.6	— 408	23.3 under
1894	Feby. 28	1872	678	332	1586	2596	724	27.9	— 286	18.
1895	Mch. 5	1965	662	329	1667	2658	693	26.2	— 298	17.8
1896	Feby. 28	1966	653	334	1648	2635	669	25.4	— 318	19.2
1897	Mch. 8	1898	642	333	1669	2644	746	29.	— 229	13.6
1898	Feby. 18	2152	628	334	1982	2944	792	27.6	— 170	8.5
1899	Feby. 4	2299	608	332	2232	3172	873	28.3	— 67	3.
1900	Feby. 13	2481	613	363	2481	3457	976	25.7		0.
1901	Feby. 5	2814	634	398	2753	3785	971	23.7	+ 61	2.2
1902	Feby. 25	3128	667	448	2982	4097	969	24.	— 146	4.9
1903	Feby. 6	3350	731	516	3159	4406	1056	25.1	— 191	5.6
1904	Jany. 22	3469	765	562	3300	4627	1158	25.1	— 169	5.1
1905	Jany. 11	3728	776	589	3612	4977	1279	26.5	— 116	3.2
1906	Jany. 29	4071	814	635	4088	5537	1466	21.3	+ 17	.41 over
1907	Jany. 26	4463	860	689	4115	5664	1201	23.2	— 348	8.4 under
1908	Feby. 14	4422	905	742	4105	5752	1330	24.4	— 317	7.7
1909	Feby. 5	4840	927	772	4699	6308	1558	25.	— 141	2.9
1910	Jany. 31	5229	960	818	5190	6608	1739	22.9	+ 39	.73
1911	Jany. 7	5402	1007	884	5113	7004	1602	23.5	— 289	5.6
1912	Feby. 20	5810	1031	927	5630	7588	1778	23.4	— 180	3.1
1913	Feby. 4	6125	1048	958	5985	7991	1866	23.9	— 140	2.3
1914	Jany. 13	6175	1057	991	6072	8120	1945	23.4	— 103	1.7
1915	Mch. 4	6499	1066	1012	7148	9226	2727	29.6	+ 649	9.9 over

TABLE No. 2.

UNITED STATES TABLE OF BALANCE SHEETS.

MILLIONS OF DOLLARS.

YEAR	CIRCU-LA-TION	SPECIE ON HAND	DIS-COUNTS AND LOANS	INDI-VIDUAL DEPOSITS	NUMBER OF BANKS	CAPITAL
1811	28	15			89	52
1815 *	45	17			208	88
1816 *	68	19			246	89
1819	35	9	73			72
1820 *	44	19		35	308	137
1830	61	22	200	55	330	145
1834	94					
1835	103	43	324	75	506	200
1836	140	40	365	83	704	231
1837	149	37	457	115 / 127	713	251
1838	116	35	525 / 485	84	788 / 829	290 / 317
1839 *	135	45	492	90	840	327
1840	106	33	462	75	901	358
1841	107	34	386	64	784	313
1842	83	28	323	62	692	260
1843	58	33	254	56	691	228
1844	75	49	264	84	696	210
1845	89	44	288	88	707	206
1846	105	42	312	96	707	196
1847	105	35	310	91	715	203
1848 *	128	46	344	103	751	204
1849	114	43	332	91	782	207
1850	131	45	364	109	824	217
1851	155	48	413	128	879	227
1854	204	59	557	188	1208	301
1855	186	53	576	190	1307	332
1856	195	59	634	212	1398	343
1857 *	214	58	684	230	1416	370
1858	155	74	583	185	1422	394
1859	193	104	657	259	1476	401
1860	207	83	691	253	1562	421
1861	202	87	696	257	1601	429
1862	183	102	646	296	1492	418
1863 *	238	101	648	393	1466	405

* PANIC YEARS

TABLE No. 3.

United States Table of Balance Sheets of the National Banks—Quarterly Statement.

MILLIONS OF DOLLARS.

YEAR	CIRCU-LA-TION		SPECIE ON HAND		LEGAL TENDERS		DIS-COUNTS AND LOANS		INDI-VIDUAL DEPOSITS		NUMBER OF BANKS		CAPITAL		SURPLUS AND UNDIVIDED PROFITS	
	MAX	MIN	MAX	MIN	MAX	MIN	MAX	MIN	MAX	MIN	MAX	MIN	MAX	MIN	MAX	MIN
1865 2ND QUAR.		66	4			72		166		183	1500		393		20	
3RD "			18		189											
4TH "	171						487									
1866 2ND "			213	19	187		500		500							
3RD "											522	1644	415		71	
4TH "	280															
1867 2ND "				9	205		603		504 558		512	1642	420		86	
3RD "																
4TH "	293					92										
1868 2ND "			20		114	84	609				532	1643	420		101	
3RD "																
4TH "	295															
1869 2ND "			29				657		580			1617	426		116	
3RD "						80										
4TH "			48													
1870 2ND "							686 688		574		511	1648	430		124	
3RD "			18	94	79				546							
4TH "	296								501							
1871 2ND "					122		725					1790	458		140	
3RD "			13			93										
4TH "	318				97											
1872 2ND "					122		831		611			1940	479		147	
3RD "			10													
4TH "	336								620							
1873 * 2ND "			16	10	97		885		656		616	1976	491		163	
3RD "	339		19			92	944		622							
4TH "	341		33													
1874 2ND "			21		103			856	540		595	2027	493		173	
3RD "						80	897									
4TH "	331						955		602							
1875 2ND "			8				984		695			2087	504		182	
3RD "																
4TH "	314					70				618						
* PANIC YEARS																

TABLE No. 4 *(No. 3 continued).*

MILLIONS OF DOLLARS.

YEAR	CIRCULATION		SPECIE ON HAND		LEGAL TENDERS		DISCOUNTS AND LOANS		INDIVIDUAL DEPOSITS		NUMBER OF BANKS		CAPITAL		SURPLUS AND UNDIVIDED PROFITS	
	MAX.	MIN.	MAX.	MIN.	MAX.	MIN.	MAX.	MIN.	MAX.	MIN.	MAX.	MIN.	MAX.	MIN.	MAX.	MIN.
1876 2ND QUAR.				21						612	2,089		499		184	
3RD "																
4TH "		291	32		90											
1877			49			66	929									
2ND "		290							659		2080		479			
3RD "				21												
4TH "						66									167	
1878			54													
2ND "				29						604						
3RD "							881		625		2053		466		165	
4TH "	303															
1879			41			64	826		598							
2ND "							814				2048		454		153	
3RD "																
4TH "	321		79			54	933		765							
1880			86													
2ND "																
3RD "		317	109	105		64	974				2090		457		159	
4TH "							1040									
1881						52			1000							
2ND "		298	128							933	2132		463			
3RD "																
4TH "	323														176	
1882				109			1100		1100	1000	2269		483			
2ND "			112													
3RD "				102			1200		1122						191	
4TH "	315					68										
1883						97										
2ND "			115													
3RD "		304								1000	2501		509		196	
4TH "																
1884 ✱			109		80		1300		1100							
2ND "			128			75					2664		524		209	
3RD "		266	167		77		1306									
4TH "									1200	1000	975					
1885				177		79										
2ND "																
3RD "						69			1200		2714		527		206	
4TH "		268							1100							
1886			171			62										
2ND "				149			1470		1152		2852		548			
3RD "									1172							
4TH "		202													212	
1887			171		79											
2ND "						73	1587		1285		3049		578			
3RD "															231	
4TH "		164		159												
1888			178		72	83										
2ND "																
3RD "											3120		588			
4TH "		151	182												246	
1889						97	81	1684		1350		3170		596		269
2ND "																
3RD "																
4TH "		126		164												
1890 ✱			171			84	1811		1436							
2ND "			178								3383		626		290	
3RD "			190													
4TH "		123														
1891						82	1832		1521							
2ND "										1483	3601		662		316	
3RD "		123	199						1575							
4TH "					100				1525							
1892 †	141		230		99		2044		1700		3711		679		330	

✱ PANIC YEARS

† FIRST QUARTER ONLY

MILLIONS OF DOLLARS.

YEAR	CIRCU-LATION MAX.	MIN.	SPECIE ON HAND MAX.	MIN.	LEGAL TENDERS MAX.	MIN.	DISCOUNTS AND LOANS MAX.	MIN.	INDI-VIDUAL DEPOSITS MAX.	MIN.	NUMBER OF BANKS MAX.	MIN.	CAPITAL MAX.	MIN.	SURPLUS AND UNDIVIDED PROFIT MAX.	M.
1892																
2ND QUAR.			239		113		2171		1765							
3RD "																
4TH "	145			209							3784		689		353	
1893																
1ST "		149				90	2161		1751		3830		688		352	
2ND "				186												
3RD "	182							1843								
4TH "			251		131					1451						
1894																
1ST "	174		259		146			1872			3777		678			
2ND "																
3RD "			169				2007		1728							
4TH "				218		119									339	
1895																
1ST "			169	220				1965			3728		662			
2ND "																
3RD "									1736							
4TH "	185				196	93	2059								340	
1896																
1ST "		187			196		1982		1687		3699		653			
2ND "						118										
3RD "																
4TH "	210					110		1893		1597					342	
1897																
1ST "	202			233						1669	3634		642			
2ND "					126											
3RD "																
4TH "		193	252			107	2100		1916						341	
1898																
1ST "		184		271	120						3594		628			
2ND "																
3RD "																
4TH "						110	2214		2225						340	
1899																
1ST "			371		116											
2ND "		199														
3RD "																
4TH "				314		101	2496		2522		3602				363	
1900																
1ST "		204		339	122											
2ND "																
3RD "																
4TH "					145		2706		2623		3942		632		403	
1901																
1ST "			309	399	164											
2ND "																
3RD "																
4TH "				369		151	3038		2964		4291		665		448	
1902																
1ST "			309													
2ND "			309		164											
3RD "																
4TH "				366		141	3303		3209		4666		714		516	
1903																
1ST "			335													
2ND "					163				3200							
3RD "																
4TH "				378		142	3481				5118		758		564	

MILLIONS OF DOLLARS.

YEAR	CIRCU-LATION MAX. MIN.	SPECIE ON HAND MAX. MIN.	LEGAL TENDERS MAX. MIN.	DISCOUNTS AND LOANS MAX. MIN.	INDIVIDUAL DEPOSITS MAX. MIN.	NUMBER OF BANKS MAX. MIN.	CAPITAL MAX. MIN.	SURPLUS AND UNDIVIDED PROFITS MAX. MIN.
04 ST QUAR.	380	453						
ND "			169					
RD "		504		3772	3707	5477	776	594
TH "								
05 ST "	424		178					
ND "		495		157				
RD "		460						
TH "				4016	3889	5833	808	632
06 ST "	498 492		175					
ND "								
RD "		459						
TH "				152 4366	4289	6199	847	687
07 ST "	543		173					
ND "								
RD "		531						
TH "				151 4678	4319	6625	901	749
08 ST "								
ND "			192					
RD "								
TH "	599 680			4840	4720	6865	921	779
09 ST "	615		198					
ND "								
RD "								
TH "		694		176 5148	5120	7006	953	825
10 ST "	667							
ND "								
RD "								
TH "		672		169 5467	5304	7204	1004	894
11 ST "	680		168					
ND "								
RD "			185					
TH "		761		5663	5536	7328	1026	930
12 ST "	704		188					
ND "		769						
RD "								
TH "				6058	5944	7420	1046	969
13 ST "	717 749		189					
ND "								
RD "								
TH "				6260	6051	7509	1059	1007
14 ST "	720	792	201					
ND "	1018			6357	6111	7493	1057	1003
RD "	848	746 534		128	7581		1065	1007
15 ST "	746	591	127	6499	6348	7599	1066	1012

last three panic years. But it is very necessary in studying this table, to bear in mind that its figures are taken from the standing of the banks at the first of the year, while the panics generally occurred later in the year : the last two, for instance in the second and fourth quarter, respectively. The third and fourth tables will give more exact figures in this connection. Table Two, dealing with State Banks, is given merely to round out our banking history as told in figures.

The increase or diminution of deposits of course reflects a confident and successful, or a panicky and impoverishing, state of general business.

The adage " buy cheap and sell dear," or its practical equivalent—so scary and imitative are investors—*Buy during the last of a selling movement and sell during the last of a buying movement*, resolves itself, we venture to repeat, into : *Buy when the decline caused by a panic has produced such liquidation that discounts and loans, after steady and long-continued diminution, either become stationary for a period,*

*or else increase progressively coincident
with a steady increase in available funds;
and sell for converse reasons.*

These conclusions are also reached by
our author through analyses of the Financial History of England, France, Prussia,
Austria, etc. These I omit as unnecessarily
wearisome to the reader since I give that
of our own country. However, I will here
quote the following: "What must be noted
is the reiteration and sequence of the same
points *(faits)* under varying circumstances,
at all times, in all countries and under all
governments," and also this table showing
all the panics and their practical coincidence
in the past eighty-five years, in

France	England	and the United States.
1804	1803	
1810	1810	
1813–14	1815	1814
1818	1818	1818
1825	1825	1826
1830	1830	1829–31
1836–39	1836–39	1837–39
1847	1847	1848
1857	1857	1857
1864	1864–66	1864
	1873	1873
1882	1882	1884
1889–90	1890–91	1890–91
1894	1894	1893–94
1897	1897	1897
1903	1903	1903
1907	1907	1907
1913	1913	1913
(approximately)	(approximately)	

Truly these thirteen panics in the three countries have been practically simultaneous and one common cause must have originated them. The only cause common to all was overtrading to such an extent that neither credit nor money were to be had, so that a forced liquidation or panic inevitably ensued.

The above table effectually does away with the theory that new tariffs are directly productive of panics. For most certainly new tariffs did not occur in England, France, and the United States just before or during all the panic years enumerated, and yet, practically simultaneously in free-trade England, high-protection France, and sometimes low-tariff, sometimes high-protection United States have panics occurred for eighty years.

But, as I have shown in a note attached to this Introduction, a new tariff or a general change of duties is apt to precipitate a panic, on account of the unsettling of business, and that the consequent shaking of credit adds its quota to the forces finally culminating in a panic cannot be doubted. As a matter of history with us, substan-

tially new tariffs have always happened to
be the immediate forerunners of a panic,
and this I believe to be true in the case of
other countries.

Why is this? Is it not because the people instinctively turn to tinkering at and
changing their chief tax—the tariff—whenever they as a whole need financial relief;
and have we not shown that such relief is
needed almost every ten years, when the
overtrading, inseparable from the development of all thriving communities has made
the call for credit impossible to grant?

A new tariff may defer, or hurry, or,
occurring simultaneously, will intensify a
panic, but it may not hope to avert one
when due: yet if its changes be very grad-
ual, fixed and long predicted, and of a nature
to bring about or confirm a judicious tariff
for revenue only, they will materially help
to put business on so firm and sound a
basis that recovery from the inevitable, and
approximately decennial panics, will be
wonderfully expedited. Thus a new tariff
is a quite accurate forewarning of a panic,
and is also to no inconsiderable extent a

contributory cause. (See foot-note on page 5, *seq.*, *Interrelations of Panics, Tariffs, and the Condition of Agriculture*, etc.; and especially what is said of the panic of 1848, on page 10.)

M. Juglar has fully analyzed the three phases of our business life into Prosperity, Panic, and Liquidation, which three constitute themselves into the business cycle, that for forty years past (that is, since the present Bank of England Act, and practically since that of the Law governing the Bank of France, both of which then increased the required specie reserve) has been of about ten years. These ten years may be apportioned roughly as follows: say, Prosperity for five to seven years; Panic a few months to a few years,[1] and Liquidation about a few years.

I have already pointed out the signs of prosperity, of panic, and of liquidation, but in view of existing conditions perhaps it

---

[1] The panic after 1873 is the only one I know extending to anything like the length it attained. This may be ascribed to the immense development and consequent speculation, and to the inflation of the currency coming after the period about the Civil War.

may be well to restate here the quite famil-
iar fact that the completion of liquidation
that precedes the beginning of another
period of prosperity is characterized by
lack of business, steady prices, and a
marked growth in available banking funds.

[The various tables spread through this
pamphlet are fully explained by their head-
ings and the text.]

In conclusion I wish to express my thanks
for the courtesy M. Juglar has extended
me, and to state my appreciation of the mo-
tives, painstaking patience, and undoubted
originality he has shown in explaining and
executing so faithfully and with such genius
a most laborious and yet spirited work. It
is only justice that such an achievement
should have been awarded a prize by the
French Institute (Academy of Moral and
Political Sciences) and have gained for M.
Juglar the Vice-Presidency of the "Society
for the Study of Political Economy."

DeCourcy W. Thom.

Wakefield Manor.

A HISTORY OF PANICS IN THE UNITED STATES CONSIDERED WITH SPECIAL REFERENCE TO AMERICAN BANKS.

THE English Colonies soon after their settlement issued paper money. The first was Massachusetts, which issued it even before her independence, in 1690, to obtain funds in order to besiege Quebec.

This example was followed to such an extent that it caused a marked speculation in favor of hard money, varying according to the quantity of notes in circulation. In 1745, after a successful campaign against Louisburg and the taking of that fortress, two million pounds of paper money were issued, which step decreased its value. When liquidation occurred these paper pounds were not worth 10 per cent. of their face value.

The War of Independence obliged Congress to issue three million of paper dollars.

This amount increased to $160,000,000, so that Congress declared, in 1779, that it would not issue more than $200,000,000. Notwithstanding this guaranty, notwithstanding the forced and legal rating conferred by this enactment, notwithstanding the war spirit, it depreciated; and in 1779 it was necessary to decree that, disregarding its normal value, it should be taken at its face.   In 1780 it was no longer taken for customs dues.   In 1781 it had no rating and was not even taken at 1 per cent. of its face value.

Between 1776 and 1780 the issue of paper money increased to $359,000,000.

Bank of North America.—In 1781 Mr. Morris, Treasurer, persuaded Congress to form a bank (the Bank of North America) with a capital of $10,000,000, of which $400,000 should be turned over to help the national finances.   The capital was too insignificant and the course of politics too unpropitious to accomplish this end.   However, the example encouraged the States to take up their paper money.   Upon the adoption of the United States Constitution the issuing of paper money ceased, and gold and silver were the only means of circulation. Thence arose great embarrass-ment for the Bank of North America, which, hampered by its loans to the Gover-ment, increased its note circulation to an enormous proportion. The ebb of paper through every channel finally aroused the public fears, and people refused the notes. Every one struggled to obtain metallic money, hence it became impossible to bor-row, and bankruptcy followed. Such was the excitement that the Philadelphians as a body demanded and obtained from the Assembly of Representatives a withdrawal of the charter; but the Bank, relying upon Congress, continued until March 17, 1787; succeeded even in extending its charter fourteen years; and later obtained a second extension, limited, however, to Pennsylvania.

The difficulty experienced in the manu-facture of money led Mr. Hamilton, Secre-tary of the Treasury, to propose to Con-gress in 1790 the founding of a National Bank. After some doubts as to the power of Congress, it was authorized. It began operations in 1794, under the title of "Bank of the United States," with a capital of ten millions, eight millions being subscribed by private individuals, and two millions by the Government. Two millions of the first sum were to be paid in metallic money, and six millions in 6 per cent. State bonds; the charter was to run till March 4, 1811. It seemed to be a good thing for the public and the stockholders, for during twenty-one years it paid an average of 8 per cent. dividends. In 1819 the question of renewing its privileges came up, the situation being as follows:

ASSETS.	LIABILITIES.
6 per cent.	Capital
Paper....$ 2,230,000	Stock....$10,000,000
Loans and	
Discounts. 15,000,000	Deposits..... 8,500,000
Cash....... 10,000,000	Circulation... 4,500,000

The profits from the Bank, the prosperous state of the country, and the increase of productions led people to think that the issuing of paper money caused it all; seduced by this alluring theory the

" Farmers' Bank " was founded in Lancaster
in 1810, with a capital of $300,000. Others
followed; such was the mania that the
Pennsylvania Legislature was forced to
forbid every corporation to issue notes.
Despite this preventive message the excitement rose so high that companies, formed
to build harbors and canals, also put notes
into circulation; in this way the law was
eluded.

From 1782 to 1812 the capital of the
banks rose to $77,258,000; upon the 1st
of January, 1811, there were already eighty-
eight banks in existence. Until the declaration of war (June, 1812),the issuing of notes
was always made with the intention of
redeeming them, but the over-issue soon
became general, and depreciation followed.
The periodical demands for dollar-pieces
for the East Indian and Chinese trade were
warnings of the over-speculations on the
part of those companies whose members
were not personally liable. Traders, who
through their notes or their deposits had
a right to credit with the banks, did
not hesitate to ask for $100,000, where-

as, formerly they would have hesitated to ask for $1,000. The war put a stop to the exportation of precious metals, which, in the ordinary course of things, limits the issue and circulation of paper. The upshot of this was to redouble the note issue, each one believing its only duty was to get the largest amount into circulation. Loans, and enormous sums of money, were distributed above all reason among individuals and among the States. The increase of dividends and the ease of obtaining them extended the spirit of speculation in certain districts, and especially among those who owned land. The remarkable results shown by the Bank of Lancaster, the "Farmers' Bank," which, by means of an extraordinary issue of notes, had yielded as much as 12 per cent. and piled up in capital twice the amount of its stock, caused it to be no longer thought of as a bank intended to assist trade with available capital, but as a mint destined to coin money for all owning nothing at all. Led by this error, laborers, shopkeepers, manufacturers, and merchants betook themselves to quitting active occupations to indulge in golden dreams. Fear alone restrained some stockholders connected with the non-authorized companies, and led them to seek for a legal incorporation.

In Pennsylvania, during the session of 1812, an act was passed authorizing twenty-five banks, with a capital of $9,000,000. The Executive nevertheless refused to ratify it, and returned it with some very well-deserved comments. In a second debate the first resolution was rescinded by a vote of 40 to 38. In the following session the proposition was renewed with more vigor, and forty-one banks with a capital of $17,000,000 were authorized by a large majority; the representations of the Executive proved useless, and they immediately entered upon their duties with an insufficient capital.

To discount their own stock was a soon-discovered method. They thus increased the amount of notes, which depreciated in comparison with hard money, and dissipated on all hands the hope of exchanging with it.

In the absence of a demand from abroad for hard money, the demand came from within our own borders.

The laws of New England, which were very severe upon the banks, had placed a penalty of 12 per cent. upon the annual interest payments of those persons who did not pay their notes. The natural result was a difference of value between New England and Pennsylvania, which measured the depreciation caused by paper in the latter district. As remittances on New England could only be made in hard money, the equilibrium of the banks was disturbed ; they were not able to respond to the demands for redemption, and a suspension of payments by the banks of the United States, except those of New England, took place in August and September, 1814.

The Panic of 1814.—An agreement took place at Philadelphia between the bank and the chief houses allied with it to resume payments at the end of the war.

Unhappily, the public did not demand the accomplishment of this promise at the time fixed, and the banks, led on by the thirst of gain, issued an unprecedented amount of bank notes. The general approbation brought about a still further increase in their number: the bank notes of the Bank of Philadelphia were at a discount of 80 per cent.; the others at 75 per cent. and 50 per cent., and metallic money disappeared to such an extent that paper had to be used to replace copper coin. The depreciation of fiat money raised the price of everything; this superficial occurrence was looked upon as a real increase, and gave rise to all the consequences that a general inflation of value could produce. This mistake on the subject of artificial wealth made landed proprietors desire unusual proceeds. The villager, deceived by a demand surpassing his ordinary profits, extended his credit and filled his stores with the highest-priced goods; and importations, having no other proportion to the real needs than the wishes of the retailers, soon glutted the market. Every one wished to speculate, and every one eagerly ran up debts. Such was the abundance of paper

3

money that the banks were alarmed lest they could not always find an investment for what they manufactured. It thus happened that it was proposed to lend money on collateral, while the greatest efforts to bring about its redemption were being made. This state of things lasted till the end of 1815, when it was recognized that the paper circulation had not enriched the community, but that metallic money had enhanced.

The intelligent portion of the nation comprehended that even where the estimated value of property had been highest, the true welfare of society had diminished. They learned too late the baleful effects of this circulation of paper money; the greater part of the States and cities had nothing to show for it.

A new class of speculators then appeared, trying to pass these worthless bank notes: forgers of paper money became more active. In the midst of this disorder a National Bank, which should afford a solid basis for the paper circulation, was considered. Influenced by these difficulties, and in hopes of remedying them, the

Secretary of the Treasury proposed to Congress, in September, 1814, a few days after suspension, to found a national bank, in order to re-establish metallic circulation, an end which the State banks had failed to accomplish.

This project, which lent the national credit to the capital of the bank, was antagonized by a good many members who exaggerated its consequences; at the same time that they took more or less important sums in bank notes, or borrowed from the banks upon the nation's guaranty, in order to re-establish the public credit and to obtain means for prolonging the war.

Causes of the Panic of 1814.—The bank directors laid the blame upon the blockade of the ports, which, interfering with, indeed even preventing, the export of products, occasioned the outflow of the metals. The national loans to carry on the war also had their influence. From the beginning of hostilities until 1814 they increased to $52,-848,000, distributed as follows: Eastern States, $13,920,000; New York, Pennsylvania, Maryland, and District of Columbia,

$27,792,000 ; Southern and Western States, $11,136,000.

Nearly all of this was advanced by the cities of New York, Philadelphia, and Baltimore. The banks made advances beyond their resources, augmenting their circulation in consequence.[1]

From the 1st of January, 1811, to the 1st of January, 1815, one hundred and

---

[1] The cause of the crisis, according to the Committee of the Senate, was the abuse of the banking system ; the great number and bad administration of the banks ; and their speculations designed to advance their stock, and to distribute usurious dividends. When the Bank of the United States saw the danger that menaced it, it reduced its discounts and circulation. The circulation of the country banks fell from $5,000,-000 to $1,300,000, and the total circulation from $10,000,000 to $3,000,000.

Increase and Decrease Circulation in Pennsylvania.

	City Banks.	Country.	Total.
1814.........	$3,300,000	$1,900,000	$5,200,000
1815.........	4,800,000	5,300,000	10,100,000
1816.........	3,400,000	4,700,000	8,100,000
1817.........	2,300,000	3,800,000	6,100,000
1818.........	1,900,000	3,000,000	4,900,000
1819.........	1,600,000	1,300,000	2,900,000

	Number of Banks.	Capital.	Circulation.	Specie.
1811........	88	$52,000 00	$28,000 00	$15,000 00
1815........	208	82,000 00	45,000 00	17,000 00
1816........	246	89,000 00	68,000 00	19,000 00

twenty new banks were registered, thus raising their capital to more than $80,000,-000; this increase took place during a war that entirely did away with foreign trade. The expenses of the war declared against Great Britain in June, 1812, were defrayed by notes issued by the banks of the various States. Six million dollars were obtained from them in 1812, in the following year, 1813, twenty million, and then fifteen million in exchange for twelve million of Federal stock, issued at the price of $125 face for every $100 paid in. Until January 1, 1814, in order to avoid taxation, Treasury bonds were issued in addition to what was contributed by the banks.

In 1812	$3,000,000
" 1813	6,000,000
" 1814	8,000,000

Up to this time no account of their administration had been rendered, but now Mr. Bland, a Maryland representative, called attention to the fact that all their operations seemed veiled from the public. Unfortunately we have been unable to find a statement of the discounts.

The suspension of specie payments differed with the corresponding state of affairs in England, inasmuch as it was not general, and, since each State was independent, the depreciation varied. It became very difficult to circulate paper, and the Government was again obliged to issue Treasury bonds, bearing 6 per cent. interest. In February, 1815, peace having been proclaimed, it was hoped that the banks would resume specie payments. There was no sign of it. The re-establishment of peace merely made some of the legal regulations seem less pressing upon the banks.

In the middle of May, 1815, the first English vessel arrived, and business became very active again. In May, June, and July it might have been said "This is the golden age of commerce." Discounts of unsecured paper were easy, and it was not an unusual occurrence to have notes of $60,000 offered.

The banks had authorized a suspension of specie payment in order to force the issue of bank notes, and to stimulate trade, although Mr. Carey pretends that no over-trading had taken place. He blames them for having restricted their loans in October and November, thus producing a decline in prices ; and the necessity of cutting down credits came about, according to him, from the speculations in National securities.

Six Philadelphia banks with a capital of $10,000,000 held $3,000,000 in Government stock.

On the 15th of February, 1815, when scarcely through with all this confusion, an effort was made to re-establish for the second time a United States Bank. It was authorized on the 10th of April, 1816, the Act permitting the formation of a Company, with a capital of $35,000,000, divided into 350,000 shares of $100 each, of which the Government took 70,000 shares and the public 180,000 shares. These last were payable in $7,000,000 of gold or silver, of the United States of North America, and $21,000,000 in like money, or, in the funded debt of the United States either in the 6 per cent. Consolidated Debt at par, the 3 per cent. at 65, or the 7 per cent. at 106½ per cent. ; upon subscription $30 was payable, of which at least $5 had to be in gold

or silver; in six months after, $35, of which
$10 had to be in metal, and twelve months
after the same amount was to be paid in the
same manner.   The directors were authorized to sell shares every year to the amount
of $2,000,000, after having offered them at
the current price to the Secretary of the
Treasury for fourteen days.   The Government reserved the right to redeem the debt
at the subscription price.

The charter, made out in the name of
the president, ran until March 3, 1836.
There were twenty-five directors of the concern, five of whom were appointed by the
President of the United States with the
consent of the Senate, and not more than
three by the State; the stockholders chose
the others.

The corporation could not accept any
inconvertible property, or any farm-mortgage, unless for its immediate use, either as
security for an existing debt, or to wipe
out a credit.

It had no right to contract any debt
greater than $35,000,000, more than its de-
posits, unless by special act; the directors

were made responsible for every violation,
and could be sued by each creditor. They
could only deal in gold and silver exchange,
and not in other country securities which
could not be realized upon at once. The
Bank could purchase no public debt nor
exceed 6 per cent. interest on its discounts
and loans. It could lend no more than
$500,000, to the United States, $50,000, to
each State, and nothing to foreigners. It
could give no bill of exchange greater than
$5,000; bank notes less than $100 were to
be payable on demand, and greater sums
were not allowed to run longer than sixty
days. Two settlements were to take place
every year.

Branches were to be established upon
demand of legislative authorities, wherever
2,000 shares of stock were subscribed for.

There were to be no bank notes less than
$5.00, and every bill of exchange, or bill
payable at sight, was to be receivable by
the public Treasury.

The duty of the Bank was especially to
pay out and receive the public money,
without profit or loss. It was to serve as

agent for every State contracting a loan; the cash belonging to the United States was to be deposited at the Bank whenever the Secretary of the Treasury did not dispose of it otherwise, in which case he was to notify Congress.

Neither the Directory nor Congress could suspend payment of the bank notes, discounts, or deposits : such refusal carried a right to 12 per cent. interest.   In exchange for this charter the Bank was to give $1,000,000, to the Government in three instalments.

The charter was exclusive during its life, excepting in the District of Columbia, where banks might be authorized, provided their capital did not exceed $6,000,000.

The Bank did not open at once, for it sent an agent to Europe to look up bullion.

Between July, 1817, and December, 1818, it thus procured $7,311,750, at an expense of $525,000.   On the 20th of February, 1817, it was decided that, excepting gold and silver and Treasury notes, no notes would be received at the Government Treasuries, save such as were payable to the banks in hard money. Notwithstanding this discrimination the banks decided not to resume specie payment until the 1st of July, 1817.

In the meantime an immense speculation had taken place in its stock, which was compromising for the Bank and for the credit of its Directory, because several of its Directors appointed by the Government took part in it. For example, it became customary to loan a very large amount of money on the Bank's own stock, as much as $125 on each share of $100. Thus more than the purchase price was loaned upon them : in furnishing the means of paying for them by credit, speculation was aroused, and on the 1st of September, 1817, the market price advanced to $156.50, at which rate it continued until December, 1818, when it fell to $110.

At last the public perceived that the excessive issue depreciated the bank-note circulation, and that a greater shrinkage was imminent.

An office for the payment of bank dividends was opened in Europe, so as to increase the price of the stock and the speculation in it through this facility, rather than for the permanent benefit of the institution. Let us note here the short-sightedness of the Directors, who thought they would stem the depreciation of their means of payment by persuading all the banks to declare what was not true, that the bank notes were worth par.

On the 21st of February, still aiming at the same end, they announced the resumption of specie payment. The State Banks, remembering the embarrassment of the public, which for two years had paid an exchange of 6 per cent., persuaded themselves that few people would dare to ask for large sums. They hoped to come to an understanding and to cause the acceptance of a promise to pay upon a designated day.

We say "a promise to pay," for this was not a serious proposition, inasmuch as foreign money and that of the United States had enjoyed a higher market value for a long time.

The depreciation of the bank notes might result just as well, from the fear of the public's enforcing its rights, as from a refusal of the banks to make good their promises. This understanding was not, properly speaking, a resumption of specie payment, but rather a kind of humbug.

In January the banks of New York, Philadelphia, Baltimore, Richmond, and Norfolk decided to resume specie payment on the 20th of February, provided the balance showing against them was not demanded by the Bank of the United States before discounts became $2,000,000, at New York, as much in Philadelphia, and $1,500,000 in Baltimore; and these conditions were accepted.

The discount line of the Bank of the United States was thus greatly increased; it grew from $3,000,000 on the 27th of February to $20,000,000 on the 30th of April; to $25,000,000 on July 29th, and to $33,000,000 on the 31st of October. The Bank imported much metallic money, redeemed its notes and those of its branches without distinction; the notes of its Eastern and Southern branches were returned as soon as those of the North had paid them, and they were newly issued; consequently eighteen months after this practice began the cash boxes of the North were drained of their capital, the length of discount was reduced, and 5 per cent. was charged for sixty days. On April 1, 1819, only $126,000, cash remained on hand, on the 12th only $71,000, remained, $196,000, was owed to the city banks.

Scarcely had the Directors of the National Bank succeeded in replacing the paper issued but not redeemed by their bank-note circulation, being fully aware from their own experience that the circulation could only reach a limited amount, than they inundated the market with it, and in a few months all reductions vanished. In this way the market price shortly resumed its former quotation, and all the difficulties reappeared. This imprudent management necessarily threw one portion of the public into debt, from which it had saved itself; and the other portion into the vortex which it had avoided. The critical moment was delayed somewhat, but the day of reckoning was near.

The Panic of 1818.—The Bank at last discovered that it had passed the bounds of safety through its issues, and that it was at the mercy of its creditors. It saw firstly, on October 21, 1818, the payment of part of the State of Louisiana's foreign debt withdraw large sums, and then Chinese, Indian, and other goods reach fancy prices because of the depreciation of the circulating medium. All these influences produced a demand for specie payment which the Bank as a public one was obliged to meet, under penalty of 12 per cent. interest, and without power to avail itself of the same accounts as the State banks.

From this moment it thought fixedly of its safety and of how to reduce its notes; this reduction obliged the other banks to imitate it, and a new crisis shook trade in the end of October, 1818. During one year the National Bank furnished from its cash boxes more than $7,000,000, and the others more than $3,000,000.

The State banks naturally followed the same policy in their connection, and their circulation became reduced as follows:

On November 1, 1816, to............$4,756,000
    "   "   "   1817, " 3,782,000
    "   "   "   1818, " 3,011,000
    "   "   "   1819, " 1,318,000

It will give a faint idea of the excessive
issue to state that the only difficulty was
the impossibility of examination by the
President and Cashier, and of their jointly
signing the notes, which was made obliga-
tory by the regulations; hence they asked
power from Congress to grant this right to
the Presidents and Cashiers of the Branch
Banks. This facility was refused, but
Congress granted a Vice-President and a
Vice-Cashier to sign. With these issues
and a simple capital of $2,000,000, the Bank
discounted as much as $43,000,000, during
one year, in addition to $11,000,000, to
$12,000,000, loaned upon public securities.

In order to carry on its operations, it exchanged in Europe a portion of its funded
debt for gold and silver, and bought specie
in the West Indies. From July, 1817, to
July, 1818, it imported $6,000,000, of specie,
at an expense of $500,000, but the exces-
sive issue of paper drained away the cash
more rapidly than the Bank could import

it. In the face of this hopeless struggle, in July, 1818, it entirely changed its course and reduced its discounts, and 10 per cent. premium was then paid for cash, and the reduction of nearly $5,000,000, in the discount line in three months only had a disastrous effect, while at the same time they would only receive for redemption the notes issued by each Branch Bank: hence general embarrassment arose, and as the Bank of the United States was withdrawing cash from the local banks, Congress wished to forbid the exportation of gold and silver. The committee appointed on the 30th of November, 1818, to examine the affairs of the Bank concluded that it had violated its charter:

1. In buying $2,000,000, of the Public Debt.

2. In not requiring from the purchasers of its stock the payment of the second and third instalments in cash, and in the Public Debt of the United States.

3. In paying dividends to purchasers of its stock who had not entirely paid up.

4. In allowing voting by proxy to a greater extent than the charter permitted.

Upon receipt of the report the Governor fled, and the shares fell to $93. In 1818 the speculation was so wild that no one failed on account of a smaller sum than $100,000. A drawing-room that had cost $40,000, and a bankrupt's wine-cellar estimated to have cost $7,000, were cited as instances of the general prodigality.

The Senatorial Committee of Inquiry declared that the panic imposed ruinous losses upon landed property, which had fallen from a quarter to even a half of its value. In consequence forced sales, bankruptcies, scarcity of money, and a stoppage of work occurred. House-rents fell from $1,200, to $450; the Federal stock alone held its own at 103 to 104.

On the 13th of December, 1819, a Committee of the House of Representatives reported that the panic extended from the greatest to the smallest capitalists. It concluded by demanding the intervention of the legislative power to restrain the corporation, which, spreading its branches throughout the Union had inundated it with nearly $100,000,000, of new circulating medium. Those who unfortunately owed money lost all the fruit of long work, and skilled laborers were obliged to exchange the shelter of their old homes for the inhospitable western forests. Forced sales of provisions, merchandise, and implements were made, greatly below their purchase price. Many families were obliged to limit their most necessary wants. Money and credit were so scarce that it became impossible to obtain a loan upon lands with the securest titles; work ceased with its pay, and the most skilful workman was brought to misery; trade restricted itself to the narrowest wants of life; machinery and manufactories lay idle; the debtor's prison overflowed; the courts of justice were not able to look after their cases, and the wealthiest families could hardly obtain enough money for their daily wants.

The Committee appointed by the Senate of Pennsylvania reported on the 29th of January, 1820, that, to prevent a bad administration of the banks, it was necessary:

1.   To forbid them to issue more than half of their capital in notes.

2.   To divide with the State all dividends in excess of 6 per cent.

3.   Excepting the president, that no director should be re-appointed until after an interval of three years.

4.   To submit to the State's inspection the bank's business and books.

From this period excessive profits and losses ceased on the part of the American banks.   The change of directory of the National Bank, called forth by the unfortunate experience of 1818, was the beginning of a very fortunate epoch.   As was always the case, business affairs resumed their usual course when liquidation ceased. Among the various causes assigned for the panic, the increase of import duties had to be pointed out, and the decrease of the Public Debt which was reduced between 1817 and 1818 more than $80,000,000.

It was impossible to turn any portion of the public deposits in proper time either into Federal stock or such other forms of value as its creditors might demand, without shaking or breaking down any respectable institution whatever. But these seem to be only secondary causes.

Panic of 1825 to 1826.—In 1824 in Pennsylvania there was a new rage for banks, and in 1825 there was a repetition of the marvellous days of 1815. American banking bubbles have always been exactly similar to the English South Sea bubble, and to Law's bank in France. In July, after an advance dating from 1819, there was a reaction, a panic, and liquidation. Here we cannot point out any of the causes which we have indicated above; the growth of trade and the exaggeration of discount sufficiently explain the difficulties of the situation.

In Pennsylvania in 1824 a bill was passed re-establishing the charters of all the banks which had failed in 1814. In New York they thought of banks alone; companies with a capital of $52,000,000 were formed. Ready money had never been so abundant, if we can judge of it by the amount of subscriptions and the great speculations in stocks.

Three millions were subscribed to the
"New Jersey Protection Company" in one
day. But in July, when the decline on
the London market was reported, the want
of hard money forced itself into notice.
Exchange on England rose from 5 per cent.
to 10 per cent.; the discount on New Orleans notes, from 3 per cent. became 50 per
cent., and on the 4th of December it had
fallen back to 4 per cent. What fluctuation ! What disasters !

Mr. Biddle, the President of the United
States Stock Bank, said that the crisis of
1825 was the most severe that England had
ever experienced, superinduced as it was
by the wild American speculation in cottons
and mines. Cotton cloth fell from 18 to
13 cents per yard ; and out of 4,000 weav-
ers employed in Philadelphia in 1825 not
more than 1,000 remained. The reaction
of liquidation was experienced in 1826, and
from 1827 money was abundant.

**Embarrassment of the Local Banks in
1828 to 1829.**—Is it necessary to mention
these embarrassments ? The trouble of 1828
affected only the local banks and not at

all those of the United States. The chief
cause was the Bank of the United States'
increase of circulation from August, 1822,
to August, 1828. From $5,400,000 it had
become $13,000,000 without adding any-
thing to the circulation, merely displacing
an equal amount of local bank notes through
drafts of branches that it put into circulation. These branch banks' drafts were in
form of bank notes, signed by the chief
employees of the branches, drawn, it might
be, on each other or on the main bank. A
great issue of paper was thus brought
about; without this roundabout method
it would have been impossible to have
forced the issue of the notes from the mere
physical inability of the president and
cashier to sign so large a number. Congress had always refused to delegate this
power to any other persons; in consequence
of this practice the inevitable result occurred in 1828, as might have been foreseen,
and a conflict between notes of the Bank
of the United States and that of the local
banks occurred.

These drafts circulated everywhere; the

branch banks received them on deposit, but did not redeem them: hence it was necessary to guard against panic by keeping hold of cash. This course increased the issue of the Bank of the United States, and of the local banks which discounted the paper of the central bank as if it were so much cash. The local banks, then, whose paper did not widely circulate, exchanged their bank notes for drafts, thus reducing the amount of circulation of the first, increasing that of the central bank, and hence that of the total issue of its bank notes; the local banks continued to exchange their paper with its narrow and limited circulation for drafts of this latter, which passed everywhere.

There occurred, then, in 1828 and 1829 an accidental and very brief scarcity of cash, whose cause we have just indicated; but since the second half of the year difficulties arising from metallic circulation had disappeared.

Panic of 1831.—The course of business, having scarcely suffered a stoppage, continued until 1831, and not till then did embarrassment occur (Oct. 8, 1831). Until then business operations were very active and money easy; the revolution in Europe rendered capital available in America, whilst the cholera and the revolution restrained the importation of foreign goods.   Discounts at the central bank rose from $24,000,000 in 1826 to $44,000,000 in 1831, and the circulation from $9,000,-000 to $22,000,000. The same increase was observable in the banks of the different States.

In March, 1830, the Bank of the United States had in its vaults $8,000,000, which was more than it had ever had before.

In 1829 the Bank of New York claimed to have so much money that it did not know what to do with it.   In 1829, 1830, 1831, the banks extended their operations, and a rise in prices accompanied the ease of getting credit; but in November, 1831, very urgent demands for money were heard.

The branch drafts, exchanged with the local banks, allowed them to increase their circulation and consequently their discounts. American writers boasted greatly about the assistance the Bank of the United States yielded both to business and the nation. Nevertheless, in 1829, President Jackson declared the conduct of the Bank to be such that its usefulness had been justly doubted by many citizens, and that the end desired, a uniform and regular circulation, had not been reached. The Senate and the House of Representatives appointed a commission that expressed an opinion contrary to that of the President.

Panic of 1837 to 1839.—In the midst of all these troubles the Secretary of the Treasury informed the President of the Bank in 1832 that the Government intended, wherever it had representatives, to redeem half of the 3 per cent. stocks by paying each holder for half of his certificates. The President answered that at that time (March 29th) this redemption from the European creditors would very greatly embarrass home business, and that therefore delay was necessary. He requested a delay of three months, because trade circles of New York had already received large advances.

The Bank, being the agent of the Treasury and having $11,600,000 on deposit, would have been forced to become a borrower in order to pay out the $2,700,000 demanded from it. However, its request was granted.

Jackson soon learned with surprise that, business being more impeded than ever, the President had despatched an agent to England to contract with the Barings a loan of $6,000,000. Seeing the Bank to be insolvent he resolved not to renew its charter. The Bank tried to hide its insolvency by the most foolish land speculations, which had already caused such great disaster in 1818 and 1820. The issue of bank notes had given fresh spirit to speculation. These bank notes were received by the National Treasury and returned to the Bank on deposit, which again loaned them to pay for land upon security of the land sold, with the result that the credit granted the Nation was merely fictitious.

In 1832, Congress having voted for the extension of the Bank's charter, President

Jackson refused to ratify it on account especially of certain changes it sought to introduce. "Why," said he, "grant a capital of $35,000,000 when the first company only had $11,000,000 ? "

But though the Bank's charter could not be arranged, the law of July 10, 1832, dealing with the regulation of banks, prescribed that "a report" upon their exact condition should be submitted to Congress every year.

In 1833 General Jackson ordered the withdrawal of the Government deposits from the Bank. The law required that the reasons for the withdrawal of the deposits should be given, and the secretary, Mr. Duane, refused to give them, saying the Bank was not insolvent. He was dismissed and replaced by a more amenable secretary. The deposits were withdrawn and placed in different State Banks. The Bank of the United States was obliged to limit its discounts and loans, thus causing trouble: however, the President wished at any loss to establish a metallic circulation.

Congress was busy through the whole session of 1833–1834 upon the withdrawal of the deposits from the Bank. The Senate sided with the Bank and condemned the President's resolution : the House of Representatives, on the contrary, approved his conduct. The Bank stopped its dealings with the Government in 1836 : the President, Mr. Biddle, whom the stockholders had complimented by presenting him a silver service, obtained through a gift of $10,000,000, whose distribution was entirely shrouded in mystery, the especial charter of the Bank of Pennsylvania. He was unwilling to render any account to Congress, notwithstanding reiterated demands. His charter terminated in 1836, and two years after he no longer had the right to transact any business.

When they had obtained the extension of the charter of the Bank of Pennsylvania, the Directors apparently gave no attention to paying their obligations to the Government ($16,000,000). They had turned over books, papers, notes, and engagements to the new corporation, which opened as a successor to the former one.

They had already put bank notes in circulation, despite a notification to redeem them, and to destroy those which remained in their hands.

President Jackson and his successor, Van Buren, considered the excessive issue of paper money as the principal cause of the panic, as well as of the overdoing of every branch of trade, of the boundless speculations, the increase of foreign debts, of imprudent land speculations, and of the alarming increase of a luxury fatal to the springs of industry and to the morality of the people. President Van Buren said that the $30,000,000 entrusted to the Bank had fostered lawless speculations. He strained every effort to reestablish metallic circulation : the banks whose notes were below $5 were no longer recognized by the National Treasury. Until the 3d of March, 1837, it was allowable to make payments with $10 notes, after that time with $20, and finally the banks were only to accept notes whose exchange was at par.

President Adams favored small paper notes of 25 to 10 cents, to the extent of $1,000,000. From 1831 to 1837, $3,400,-000 twenty-five cent notes, $5,187,000 ten-cent notes, and $9,771,000 five-cent notes were issued. To prevent an abuse of this it was necessary to resume a metallic circulation immediately. In 1833 the amount of small notes issued had already reached $37,000,000; in 1837 it became $73,000,000; it even exceeded these figures; it was this circulation of small paper notes that had to be made smaller than $120,000,000.

Notwithstanding these frequent panics the national prosperity and the increase of wealth were unquestionable and astonished all observers.

From 1817 to 1834 the national expenses diminished from $39,000,000 to $24,000,-000, decreasing even to $14,000,000 in 1835, while the income grew to $37,000,000.

From 1826 to 1836 the condition of business, despite the panic of 1831, grew easier. Industries, agriculture, and commerce were prosperous and every enterprise was successful. Both in New Orleans and in New York there was much building, and more than 1508 houses were erected between January 1 and September 1, 1836. This general prosperity carried with it the seeds of trouble.

The rapid increase of the National revenue gave birth to the belief that capital had increased in the same proportion. This superabundance of income produced temporarily by the inflation in business was recklessly thrown away. People speculated in land, projected a hundred railroads, canals, mines, and every sort of scheme, which would have absorbed $300,-000,000 if carried out.

The national capital being insufficient, loans were made in England and Holland, where the rate of interest being more moderate stimulated the passion for enterprises. Finally, in order to stop the flow of English capital to America, the Bank of England raised the rate of interest; this brought people to their senses. They saw the impossibility of carrying out a third of their schemes. Cotton fell, and panic seized the public.

Since 1818 a period of flow and ebb in trade had been seen every five or six years, but this stoppage was much more serious. The lack of ready money and capital destroyed confidence. Money was not to be had upon any collateral; and the banks stopped discounting. The people lacked bread, the streets were deserted, the theatres empty; social observances were in abeyance, there were no more concerts, and the whole social round was stopped.

The Bank of the United States used various expedients to temporarily moderate the crisis until the very moment that it burst all the more violently in 1839, and brought about a new and radical reform.

From the time that the separation of the Bank of the United States from the Government and the cessation of its operations as the National Bank was brought about, the quotation on bank notes considerably decreased, as well for those payable at sight as for the deferred notes payable in twelve months. The President sent an agent to London to raise money upon the bank shares.

Fearing that General Jackson would not establish a new bank, and by way of counterpoise, one hundred banks were created with a capital of more than $125,000,000; issues of bank stock were not to exceed three times the amount of the capital, but this provision was not observed; the issue was without regulation and without limits, and during an inflation in prices of the necessaries of life which had doubled in value, and which had turned the people's attention to agriculture. The price of land had for some time advanced tenfold, and the advance in cotton caused the Southern planters to abandon indigo and rice.

Imports in 1836 exceeded the exports by $50,000,000, which had to be paid in gold or silver. This outflow of metal created a great void.

The advance in the discount rate in the Bank of England under such circumstances came like a thunder-clap, and the distended bladder burst. Banks suspended payment, and bank notes lost from 10 to 20 per cent. Exchange on France and England rose to 22 per cent., all metal disappeared from circulation, and a thousand failures took place. The English export houses lost from £5,000,000 to £6,000,000 sterling; values fell from maximum to minimum. The losses in America were even greater; cotton fell to nothing. At the worst of the panic people turned to the Bank of the United States, and its President, being examined as to the means of remedying the trouble, stated that it was above all necessary to maintain the credit of the Bank of England in stead and in place of private credit, which had disappeared. He proposed to pay everything in bank paper on Paris, London, and Amsterdam.

When the panic came the Bank was very much shaken. At the beginning of April, 1837, the New York banks suspended payments because demands for hard money for export played the chief rôle; the other banks suspended in their turn, promising to resume with them.

The Bank of the United States suspended also, Mr. Biddle, the President, asserting that it would have continued to pay were it not for the injury done by New

York. This was false, for the New York
banks shortly after resumed payment, hop-
ing they would be imitated, but the other
banks refused to do so. Mr. Biddle wished,
in the first place, to await the result of the
harvest. To uphold the Bank, he tried to
bring about exchanges, both with banks
and general business, not only in America
but in Europe, in order to establish a unity
of interests which would sustain him and
conceal his real condition. In this he was
successful to a certain degree, for in 1840
in his balance sheet $53,000,000 of paper
of the different States was shown up. He
wished above all to secure the monopoly
of the sale of cotton: a senseless speculation hitherto unexampled,[1] the like of
which may never be seen again.

Whilst the Bank came to the relief of
New York business through its exchange
and its deferred notes, Biddle posed as
the great cotton agent, on condition that
the Bank's agents should be consigned to
at Havre and Liverpool. In their embar-

---

[1] A similar episode has occurred in our time in the speculation in metals by the "Comptoir d'Escompte."

rassment this proposition was accepted by the planters. Cotton was thus accumulated in those two places. This monopoly advanced the price, and vast sums were realized, which enabled him to enlarge the scope of his business. In 1837 he was enabled by this means to draw on London for £3,000,000 sterling; the difference between 5 to 6 per cent. interest and discount at 2 per cent. produced a very handsome profit. The cotton merchants prospered as well as the exchange agent, and Mr. Biddle paid the planters in bank notes which the Bank could furnish without limit, while he received in Europe hard money for the cotton; this aroused opposition.

In the second half of 1837 he established in Missouri, Arkansas, Alabama, Georgia, and Louisiana a number of new banks, to make advances to the planters, and to sell their products for them in Europe. They started with very slight capital, they observed no rules in issuing paper, their bank notes fell 30 per cent. in 1838, and the planters would not take them.

The Bank of the United States, fearing
lest foreign capitalists should take advantage of the difficulties of the planters by
buying this cotton, cheapened on account
of the encumbrances upon the district producing it, resolved to come to the rescue of
the Southern banks, and to join them in
their operations by purchasing their shares
and their long-time paper, having two
years to run. It thus put $100,000,000
into the business, and in 1838 it had loaned
them upon their cotton crops not less than
$20,000,000 at 7 per cent., payable in three
years.

It had bought the bank shares at 28 per
cent. below par; through its help they
had risen again to par; and then it threw
them upon the London market, which absorbed them. In order to explain the immense credit enjoyed in Europe by the
United States and their banks, we must
observe that the extinguishment of the
National obligations through surplus crops
threw a false light upon the credit of the
States, as well as particularly upon that of
the corporation. For many years Amer-

ican investments had been sought for above all others in London, and as nothing happened during the first year to destroy that confidence, the amount thus employed increased from $150,000,000 to $200,000,-000 in 1840. In Pennsylvania $16,000,000 of European money was used in the Bank of the United States, and $40,000,000 in those of the different States, all of which was payable in two or three years.

Mr. Biddle had succeeded in sustaining the different States with the National credit. He knew how to utilize the credit of American goods in Europe, and drew from the London market an immense sum against exchange long-time paper and paper payable in America. The Bank's paper fell from 4 to 6 per cent., and it was in such demand that the Bank of England took it at 2 to 3 per cent. discount. But finally the market had all that it could take. The attention of merchants was attracted to Mr. Biddle's gigantic speculations, who paid paper in America and collected hard money in London. Business interests complained about the contraction in the market. The Bank's stock of cotton increased steadily, and between June and July it rose from fifty-eight to ninety million bales.

This speculation had already yielded $15,000,000 profit, but the market was overloaded, and quotations could not keep up. The planters had made a great deal by the advance in cotton, but the paper money remitted them lost from 15 to 25 per cent. A panic was approaching. The cotton crop, amounting to 400,000 bales, was one fifth less than was expected; they awaited an advance in price, but the contrary occurred. The high prices had brought out all the stored cotton; the factories had reduced their work. Nevertheless bale after bale was forwarded to Liverpool and to Havre. The sale in this last port in February and March, 1839, having produced a loss, they continued to store it. As soon as Mr. Biddle was aware of this stoppage he sought to hide the difficulty by extending his business. He proposed to start a new bank in New York (the other had headquarters in Philadelphia) with a capital of $50,000,000. He once more issued long-time paper, and bought with American paper canals, rail-roads, and shares which he threw upon the English market. This lasted until the long-time paper lost 18 per cent. in America, and until American exchange and investments were no longer received on the Continent.

The Parisian house of Hottinguer like its other agents, sold little until the first of July, and when it saw that the effort to monopolize cotton could not succeed, fear-ing to continue this gigantic operation, it declared that it employed too much capital. In the midst of all this, some new bills of exchange reached Paris without consign-ment of corresponding value; and the house of Hottinguer protested.

Hope of Amsterdam discontinued his connection. The London agent called upon the Bank of England for help, which was granted upon the guaranty of certain firms of that place and a deposit of good Ameri-can paper.

Rothschild accepted the refused bills of

exchange, after having found out that a sum of £400,000 would suffice for Mr. Biddle's agent; these £400,000 offered as a guaranty consisted of Government stock, and of shares in railroads, canals, and banks. This agreement was not given out freely, which still further increased the feeling of distrust. A crisis in which $150,000,000 of European capital were destined to be engulfed was rapidly approaching.

Breaking out of the Panic of 1839.—The English papers had already warned the people to be distrustful. The *Times* said it was impossible to have any confidence in the Bank as long as it would not resume specie payments. Mr. Biddle defended himself through papers paid for the purpose, finally in the Augsburg *Gazette*, while he waited for the soap bubble to burst. His retained defenders claimed that the 150,000 bales of cotton sent to Europe had not been sold, but received on commission. Advances in paper had been made which in the month of August, 1839, were to be paid in notes by the Southern banks, for a new grant made to the Bank

by the State of Pennsylvania permitted it
to buy the shares of other banks, and by
this means to gain their management;
their notes lost 20 to 50 per cent. as compared with the Northern banks.

Through his profit upon the difference of
the notes, and through the payment for the
cotton in paper, and through the sale of
bullion exchange, Mr. Biddle had made five
to six million dollars, which lay at his com-
mand in London.

The protection of his bills of exchange
made a great impression in England; the
rebound was felt in America, where the
panic, moderated in 1837 through the intervention of the Bank, burst forth with
renewed fury in 1839, and brought about
the complete liquidation of that establish-
ment.

At the same time the English market
was very much pressed, for, according to a
notice of the Chamber of Commerce, the
number of that year's bankruptcies was
greater than usual. From June 11, 1838
to June, 1839, there were 306 bankruptcies
in London, and 781 in the "provinces,"—in

all, 1,087. At Manchester there were 82, at
Birmingham 54, at Liverpool 44, at Leeds
33. The London Exchange was flooded
with unsalable paper, an occurrence which
had also taken place on a smaller scale in
1837.

Such was the interruption of business
that interest for money rose to 20 per cent.,
and the discount rate for the best paper to
15 or 18 per cent.

The various States in the Union had
contracted debts with inconceivable ease,
and interest payments were provided for
by new loans. President Jackson declared it necessary to make a loan in order
to pay interest moneys. It was deemed
inexpedient to impose new taxes to provide for the cost of the public works.
Great was the embarrassment in America,
and as no more money came from England,
it was necessary for the Americans to look
for it in their own country.

Business circles were flooded with long-
time paper running at a discount of one
half of 1 per cent. a month. Discount
rose to 25 per cent. The panic was so

great that all confidence was destroyed.
The Bank of the United States, in order
to maintain its credit, paid its depreciated
long-time paper.

The struggle between the Bank and its
opponents, led by President Van Buren,
re-commenced. These last declared that
the Bank had erred in circulating the
$4,000,000 of notes of the old bank, which
should have been retired coincidently with
the charter; and the Senate forbade their
circulation.

The Government claimed large sums
from the Bank, the statement of which
showed close to $4,000,000; and, as it
could not secure this amount in money, it
was decided to issue $10,000,000 of Treas-
ury bonds. The Bank party wished to
push the Government into bankruptcy, in
order to induce it to turn to them for help,
and, through the issue of "circular specie,"
oblige it to adopt a system of paper money.

A bill was brought forward with this
view. Biddle, who wished to increase the
circulation, said he could resume specie
payments, and thus forced his shares to

rise; but the rejoicing of the Bank party was soon disturbed by the fact that collectors of taxes were forbidden to receive any bank note for less than $20, which was not redeemable in hard money.

After a struggle of eight years the separation became complete, and the administration of National finances was withdrawn from the Bank.

In 1836, a law was passed providing that upon the expiration of its charter, the National funds should be again deposited with it, as soon as the Bank resumed specie payment. Upon the suspension in 1837, the Government was forced to abate the law, in order to protect the specie, and imposed on its financial and postal agents some of the duties of the Treasury. In 1840, the management of the public Treasury constituted a separate and distinct department. Such was the liquidation following the panic, that Congress granted the Bank three months in which it must either resume specie payment or liquidate. To conform to this decree the State of Pennsylvania fixed the resumption of specie payments by its banks, for January 15, 1841. The shares of the Bank, which had yielded no dividend in 1839, and offered a similar outlook for the first half of 1840, fell to $61. They had been quoted as high as $1,500. General liquidation and a loss of 50 per cent. was inevitable. This occurred in 1841. Thus ceased for a time the bank mania in the United States.

We will recall here Buchanan's opinion about the Bank: "If the Bank of the United States, after ceasing to be a national bank, and obtaining a new charter in Pennsylvania, had restrained itself to legitimate banking, had used its resources to regulate the rate of home exchange, and had done everything to hasten the resumption of specie payments, it would have resurrected the National Bank.

"But this is no longer possible; it has defied Congress, violated the laws, and is mixed up in politics. The people have recognized the viciousness of its administration; the President, Mr. Biddle, has concluded the work Jackson began."

Tables indicating the banks which suspended during the panic : In 1814, 90 ; in 1830, 165 ; in 1837, 618 ; in 1839, 959.

The last panic, from 1837 to 1839, produced, according to some pretty accurate reports of 1841, 33,000 failures, involving a loss of $440,000,000.

Panic of 1848.—The entire discounts, which had risen to $525,000,000 in 1837, fell to $485,000,000 in 1838, only to rise again to $492,000,000 in 1839, and the real liquidation of the panic occurred only then.   Discounts fell at once to $462,000,-000, then $386,000,000 ; the abundance of capital, and the low price at which it was offered, cleared out bank paper until it was reduced from $525,000,000 to $254,-000,000 in 1843.[1]

The metallic reserve increased from $37,000,000 to $49,000,000 (1844); the circulation was reduced from $149,000,000 to $58,000,000.

The number of banks in 1840, from 901 fell to 691 in 1843, and the capital itself

[1] We have not the outside figures, the maximum or minimum.

from $350,000,000 in 1840 was reduced to
$200,000,000 in 1845 and to even $196,-
000,000 in 1846.

All these figures clearly indicate liquidation. The market, freed from its exchange,
was enabled to permit affairs to resume
their ordinary course.

In fact an upward movement was taking
place. Discounts rose from $264,000,000
to $344,000,000 in 1848.

Banks increased from 691 in 1843 to
751 in 1848, and their capital grew from
$196,000,000 in 1846 to $207,000,000.
The paper circulation rose from $58,000,-
000 to $128,000,000 in 1848. Deposits
from $62,000,000 reached $103,000,000 in
1848. The metallic reserve alone fell from
$49,000,000 in 1844 to $35,000,000 in
1848.

The consequences of the European panic
were felt in America, but without causing
much trouble. The liquidation of the
panic of 1839 was barely over, and was
still too recent to have permitted sufficient
extension of business

Embarrassments were slight and brief;
6

discounts, nevertheless, fell from $344,000,-
000 to $332,000,000.

The store of bullion, in spite of the surplus and the favorable balance produced
by the export of grain to Europe, fell from
$49,000,000 to $35,000,000; with the following year the forward movement recom-
menced.

Panic in 1857.—The stoppage in 1848
was very brief. Discounts rose regularly
from $332,000,000 to $364,000,000, $413,-
000,000, $557,000,000, $576,000,000, $634,-
000,000, and finally $684,000,000 in 1857.
The progression was irresistible. The circulation rose from $114,000,000 to $214,-
000,000. The banks increased at such a
rate that, from 707 in 1846, with a capital
of $196,000,000, there were in 1857 1416,
whose capital had risen to $370,000,000,—
a very inferior figure, in comparison to the
number of banks, to that of 1840, when
901 banks only had a capital of $358,-
000,000.

The metallic reserve, from $35,000,000
in 1847, easily reached $59,000,000 in
1856: but it was in proportion neither

with the number of the banks nor their discounts and circulation ; and, after all, this is only a moderate sum. We have not the extreme maximum or minimum, and the suspension of specie payments took place notwithstanding the amount of cash on hand, which was greater in 1857 than in 1856.

Deposits accumulated from $91,000,000 to $230,000,000 ; they rose to their greatest height in the very year of the crisis ; nevertheless, they could not be drawn out.

During the Eastern war the prosperity of the United States had been so great that the clearing-houses established in New York in 1853, and in Boston in 1855, offered only a slight opposition to the excessive issue : at least, in 1837 the Congressional report stated the cash on hand was $6,500,000—that is to say, $1.00 in metal to each $6.00 in paper.

In 1857 cash on hand was $14,300,000, or $1.00 in hard money for each $8.00 in paper.

The banks had attracted deposits by high interest, and loaned the money to wild speculators. On the 22d of August,

1857, the amount of loans had become almost $12,000,000, counting together metal, notes, and deposits.

From December, 1856, to June, 1857, they had shown great strength. Discounts had risen from $183,000,000 to $190,000,-000 in June ; cash on hand had risen from $11,000,000 to $14,000,000. The only evidence of weakness, so to speak, was that the withdrawal of deposits had risen from $94,000,000 to $104,000,000, while the circulation diminished $1,000,000.

In June "the position of the Bank ought not to have caused any fear, to the most far-sighted," says the report of the Committee of Inquiry.

Foreign exchange was favorable, and it is known that is the bankers' guide. June, July, and August were tranquil, except for a slight disturbance in business experienced by the country bankers through the constantly increasing amount of notes presented for redemption, and among the city bankers by requests for discount.

The collapse of the " Ohio Life," which had the best New York connection, was the first muttering of the storm, and was soon followed by the suspension of the Mechanics' Banking Association, one of the oldest banks in the country. The suspension of the Pennsylvania and Maryland banks followed. Public confidence remained unshaken — it relied upon the circulating medium.

Only one bank went to protest, and that on September 4th, on a $250 demand. Another protest followed on the 12th, a third on the 15th, both for insignificant amounts. Demands in the way of withdrawal amounted to almost nothing, and there was nothing like a panic.

The deposits at the savings banks were a little less, but this did not continue. Only at the close of September was the demand by the country banks for payment upon the Metropolitan American Exchange Bank for payment greater than it had ever been.

On the 13th of October, with exchange at par, an abundant harvest, with a premium of $\frac{1}{4}$ to $\frac{1}{2}$ per cent. on metal, the banks suspended specie payment, but resumed it on the 11th of December. The most critical period lasted about a month. The first step towards resumption of payments was made after the resolution adopted by the Committee of Liquidation to call upon the country banks to redeem the notes of the Metropolitan Bank, paying an allowance of $\frac{1}{4}$ of 1 per cent. interest, running from the 20th of November.

At this time the city bankers held, in bills issued and in signed parcels of $5,000 each, about $7,000,000 due by the country banks. They were thus enabled to accomplish the payment of their notes at the rate of 20 per cent. a month by the 1st of January, 1858. The same favor of repaying their notes at the rate of 6 per cent. was granted to the city banks.

We need not inquire if, having granted this delay, the banks proved their liberality. The abundant harvest also assisted liquidation.

From 1853 to 1857 the metallic reserve fell to $7,000,000, deposits rose to $99,000,000, and discounts and loans to $122,000,000.

BANKS OF NEW YORK.

Metallic Reserve.	Deposits.	Discounts, Advances.	Proportion of the Metallic Reserve to Deposits.
1854....$15,000,000	$ 58,000,000	$ 80,000,000	26 %
1855.... 9,900,000	85,000,000	101,000,000	11 %
1856.... 10,000,000	100,000,000	112,000,000	10 %
1857.... 7,000,000	99,000,000	122,000,000	7 %

The reduction of the metallic reserve, increase of deposits and of discounts and of advances, are here clearly indicated.

From 1853 to 1857 the bank circulation hardly varied $100,000, indicating that the demand for hard money came from abroad and from the interior. The circulation was not the cause of the suspension,—at least such was the opinion expressed by the superintendent of the New York banks in his report.

In 1856 twenty-five companies were started, and three bankers opened business with a capital of $7,500,000, of which $7,200,000, was paid in.

In 1857 there were only five of these banks and three bankers having a capital of $6,000,000, of which only $4,000,000 were paid in. The collateral deposited by the banks represented $2,500,000 in 1856, on which credit of $2,000,000 in notes was granted.

In 1857 the same collateral did not exceed $560,000 estimated value, on which a credit of $383,000 in paper was granted.

At the height of the crisis failures were so numerous that a general suspension of payments, and, in consequence, a stoppage of business was dreaded. This suspension, in place of being general, turned out to be merely partial; it occurred at a juncture when it might well be feared that it would lead on to the very greatest disasters, but, far from harming, it helped the market. The banks had suspended payment upon a common understanding among themselves and with business circles. The critical moment having passed, tranquillity reappeared as soon as the course determined on was known.

If suspension of payment hurts the credit of a bank, it does not necessarily lead to the depreciation of its bank notes.

There are a good many proofs of this: in 1796, when the Bank of England suspended, its bank notes did not depreciate; and if this state of things did not last, the blame must be laid upon the excessive issue. And in France, in 1848 as well as in 1871, the Bank of France suspended without the depreciation of its bank notes becoming very noticeable. So, in New York, bank notes passed at 2 or 3 per cent. loss at this crisis.

The crisis disappeared with the end of the year, and resumption of payments took place between New York and Hamburg, with the return of specie and a rate of 4 per cent.

It was the same in France and England. A more serious panic and a more rapid recovery had never been seen. The rigidness and not the severity of the pressure that had to be exercised shows the condition of business. There had been most blamable practices employed ; but the market as a whole was sound, and had faced the storm.

Only four banks had suspended, three of which were shaky before the panic, and the fourth had already resumed payments.

At no other period could one have ob-

tained such an amount of credit upon a
simple paper circulation; fictitious paper
was the source of all the wrecks. To get
it into circulation the most varied contri-
vances were resorted to, and fraud itself
was not wanting; the signatures even became fictitious, their owners could not be
found. Shams and discriminations under
all forms, designed to permit speculation
without capital, without exchange of goods,
without real transactions between the
drawer and the acceptor of the bill of
exchange, were rife.

In his message, President Buchanan
ascribed the crisis to the vicious system of
the fiduciary circulation, and to the ex-
travagant credits granted by the banks,
although he was aware that Congress had
no power to curb these excesses. When
there is too much paper, when the public
has created an endless chain of bank notes,
representing no real value, it is enough that
the first ring break for the whole gear, thus
no longer held together, to fall to pieces.

If we mark the situation of the New
York banks before and during the panic—

that is to say, in 1852 and in 1857, we will ascertain as follows :

	June, 1852.	June, 1856.	June, 1857.
Capital	$ 59,700,000	$ 92,300,000	$107,500,000
Circulation......	27,900,000	30,700,000	27,100,000
Deposits	65,600,000	96,200,000	84,500,000
Paper discounted	127,000,000	174,100,000	170,800,000
Cash on hand...	13,300,000	18,500,000	14,300,000

This table demonstrates that two items show a great increase : capital increased $47,000,000 and paper discounted $43,000-000 ; while, in face of an increase of $1,000,000 of specie on hand, the note circulation decreased $800,000.

Far from finding a mistake, we find a proof of the Directors' prudence. If there was an error in the issuing of paper, it was not on the side of the banks ; it was the public itself that was chiefly in fault.

We find the causes of the panic in the issues of railway obligations and shares, which had chiefly been placed in European markets, and whose gross amount was estimated at £1,000,000. The speculation in land and railroads had been carried on either with borrowed money or by open credits, and by accommodation notes, back of which there was no second party.

The mistake of the banks was in trying to conduct their whole business by their note circulation and to concentrate their capital in the bank offices, and meanwhile, as they refused to loan to the stockholders of the banks, discounts in New York fell off $10,000,000. Finally the capital could not be entrusted to the disposal of the banks and it was necessary to compel them to make a deposit of $100,000 for each association, and $50,000 for each banker.

Such were the final advices given by the inspector-general of the banks of New York at the close of his report, dealing with how to prevent the recurrence of panics. To have confidence in their efficacy, it was necessary to forget the past and its lessons.

The reforms already made and those still asked for in the bank system could yield no remedy for those abuses lying beyond legislative action. The American newspapers did not hesitate to demand them, well aware that they would produce no effect; however, they congratulated themselves with having drawn away from effete

Europe one million sterling now realized upon the soil of the United States without any equivalent given for it to the foreign lenders.

Panic of 1864.—The crisis of 1864 was mixed up in the United States with the War of Secession ; it was a political crisis, and is not properly to be considered here.

Panic of 1873.—During the last two months of 1872 the American market had been very much embarrassed ; the lowest rate of discount was 7 per cent., and in December it was quoted at even $\frac{1}{32}$ of 1 per cent. or a quarter of 1 per cent. a day !

The year 1873 was anxiously awaited in hope of better times. In the middle of January, 1873, the rate of interest declined a little to 6 or 7 per cent., but soon the rate of $\frac{1}{32}$ of 1 per cent. per day reappeared and continued until the month of May.

In the first days of April the market was in full panic ; it grew steadier in the first week of May, and in the month following. It relapsed on September 1st, and requests for accommodation redoubled until the sharpest moment of the panic. On that day there were no quoted rates; money could not be had at any price: some few loans were made at 1½ per cent. per day.

This panic broke forth on September 18th, through the failure of Jay Cooke, after a miserable year, during which money was constantly sought for and was held at very high prices in all branches of business. As to the loans for building railroads, they followed one another so rapidly that, from the month of October, 1871, to the month of May, 1873, they could not be placed at a lower rate than 7 per cent. Bankers succumbed beneath the burden of their unsalable issues. This was a grave misfortune for the railroads. In the single year 1873 there were constructed 4,190 miles of railroad in the United States, which, at $29,000 per mile, represented the enormous sum of $121,000,000, and in the last five years $1,700,000,000.

The commercial situation was not so bad, and the number of failures did not reach the proportion that might have been feared.

After the failure of Jay Cooke came those of Fiske & Hatch, of the Union Trust Company, of the National Trust Company, and of the National Bank of the Commonwealth. On the 20th of September, for the first time, the Stock Exchange in New York City was closed for ten days, during which legal-tender notes were at a premium of ¼ per cent. to 3 per cent. above certified cheques.

On the 18th there was a run on the deposits. Withdrawals continued on the 19th and 20th, especially by the country banks, and the banks' correspondents. No security could be realized upon; and in order to relieve the situation the Secretary of the Treasury bought $13,500,000 of National 5-20 bonds, stating that he could do no more.

The New York Stock Exchange was reopened September 30th, without any notable occurrence; but everything was very low. Several other suspensions occurred— for instance, that of Sprague, Claflin, & Co.

The rate of discount being 9 per cent., a panic was feared in London. The banks passed the most critical period on October 14th; out of $32,278,000 legal-tender dollars at the beginning of the panic, only $5,800,000 remained on hand. Not until the middle of November did the decline stop and a slight advance take place.

Throughout the panic the bank reserves were much below the legal requirement of 25 per cent.; from the 13th to the 20th of September they fell to 24.44 and 23.55 per cent.

The New York Clearing House in September adopted a measure which permitted dealings to continue. It authorized the banks to deposit the bills on hand, or the other securities they had accepted, in exchange for which they issued certificates of deposit bearing 7 per cent. in notes of $5,000 to $10,000 to the extent of 70 per cent. of the security deposited. Thus $26,-565,000 of them were put into circulation.

Furthermore, they made a common fund of the legal tenders belonging to the Associated Banks for mutual aid and protection.

The suspension of payment took place first in New York and then extended to the large cities of the Union; it lasted forty days, until the 1st of November; this measure was looked upon as having prevented the greatest disasters.

The table setting forth the situation, compared with the balance sheets of the Associated Banks of New York on January 1st, April 1st, July 1st, September 1st, and October 1st of the years 1870, 1871, 1872, and 1873, shows us the following changes: discounts had fluctuated from $250,000,000 in January, 1870, to $309,000,000 in September, 1871; they had become reduced to $278,000,000 in September, 1873, on the eve of the panic, and from the month of September, liquidation of the panic having begun, they were reduced to $250,000,000. Deposits from $179,000,000 in January, 1870, rose to $248,000,000 in July, 1871, with $296,000,000 of bills discounted, and once more reached $198,000,000 in September, 1873, with $278,000,000 of discounts and $195,000,000 in December.

Even at the most critical moment of the panic they continued larger than the usual average of the preceding years.

7

The metallic reserves played too feeble a role to have caused failure; they had varied from $34,000,000 in June, 1870, to $9,000,-000 in September, 1871, $18,000,000 in September, 1873, and $23,000,000 in December, 1873.

The circulation varied still less: from $34,000,000 in January, 1876, it decreased to $27,000,000 in July, 1872, and remained at the same figure during the year 1873, if we can judge of this by the balance sheet rendered on the first day of each quarter. In each case there is no opportunity for us to charge an excessive issue.

According to the statement of the Comptroller of the Currency, paper discounted decreased between the 12th of September and the 1st of November from $199,000,000 to $169,000,000.

To sum up, the circulation had fluctuated very little; deposits from $99,000,000 had increased to $167,000,000 between the 12th and 20th of September, at the most critical period; and when suspension was universal, they had declined to $89,000,000. After the breaking out on the 18th of October, and since then from the 22d of November, they had risen to $138,000,000.

The metallic reserve, after a brief revival from $14,000,000 to $18,000,000 between the 12th and 20th of September, had fallen back to $10,000,000, only to rise to $14,-000,000 in November.

In the midst of these difficulties, the securities of the various States held up. Since the first months of 1873, the demands of the English market caused an upward movement in them; in September it was impossible to make a loan, without using them as collateral. In order to help the market somewhat, the Treasury bought about $13,000,000 of National securities on the Stock Exchange, but, lacking resources, that was the only effort it could make. The German Government invested quite a large sum in the new five per cents, so that the advance in public securities lasted through the whole year: the market rate for 5–20's advanced from 91 per cent. in April to 96 per cent. in October, in the midst of the market's panic.

The $15,000,000 of indemnity awarded by

the Geneva Court of Arbitration, and paid
by England for having admitted privateers
into her ports, was put into 5–20's.   Apart
from this strength in the public securities,
the railway obligations, especially those
upon new roads, were very much depressed;
they could no longer be placed, ninety new
companies having stopped paying their
coupons, whilst those of the old lines held
their quotations.

Great speculators, Vanderbilt at the
head, formed syndicates, embracing several
companies, and made prices as suited their
plans.   The death of Mr. Clarke in June
dealt the first blow to this combination, and
the failure of George Bird Grinnell brought
about its dissolution.

The liquidation of this tremendous concern kept down prices for a long time.

The price of gold, still quoted at 112½
per cent. in January, 1873, rose to 119½ per
cent. in April, superinduced by speculation,
for at the height of the panic it declined to
106 on the 6th of November.   It is true
that at that time all doubtful accounts were
liquidated, and demands for gold had dis-

appeared; if we were to rely upon the export figures only, we would find them less
than in the preceding years.

Exchange rates were much more depressed; from 109.45, representing par, they
fell to 107.25 for the best 60-day paper.
This paper was much sought after by speculators, who, when discounting it, procured
bonds authorizing them to transfer the
titles unless payment was made promptly
at maturity. Prices fell so low that it was
often impossible to negotiate paper at any
price. The activity reigning at the beginning of the year showed itself in the Exchange movement; the excess of imports
over exports rose in the first months to
$100,000,000, whilst in the preceding year
it did not exceed $62,000,000; prices ruling
in the American market attracted goods
from all quarters.

Panic of 1884.—The panic which burst
upon the United States in 1884 was
the last thunder-clap of the commercial
tempest which had reigned since the month
of January, 1882. Public opinion already
recalled the decennial period which sepa-

rated the existing panic from that of 1873. The acute period was of short duration; the crash occurred on May 14th, and the decline of values had touched bottom by the end of June. From the 9th of June the people began to steady up, they felt the ground firmer under their feet. The situation gave evidence of great strength; and, notwithstanding the dearness of money, and an enormous fall in prices, there were only a few failures, and at the close of the year equilibrium was re-established, although the liability of the losses had risen to $240,000,000. These losses, it is true, were almost entirely borne by financiers and speculators, rather than by manufacturers and traders.

The month of May, 1884, concludes the prosperous period which followed the crisis of 1873. During this period the most gigantic speculations in railroads occurred; the zenith of the movement was in 1880, and as early as 1881 a retrograde movement began, only to end in the disasters in question. The decline in prices had been steady for three years; they had sunk

little by little under the influence of a ruinous competition, caused by the number of
new lines and the lowering of rates, but
above all through the manipulations by
the managers on a scale unexampled until
now. In connection with the disasters of
May, 1884, the names of certain speculators
who misused other people's money, such as
Ward, of Grant & Ward; Fish, President
of the Marine Bank; and John C. Eno, of
the Second National Bank, will long be re-
membered. General Grant, who was a silent
partner in Ward's concern, was an innocent
sufferer, both in fortune and reputation.

The Marine Bank suspended on the 5th
of May, and in the following week the
Metropolitan drew down in its train a large
number of bankers and houses of the second order. The confusion was then at its
height. Owing to the very delicate mech-
anism of the credit circulation, the banks
and the clearing house were the first
attacked and the most shaken, but they
immediately formed themselves into a syndicate to resist the storm which was upset-
ting all about them. As cheques were no

longer paid, settlements no longer took
place, and the credit circulation was suspended; this stoppage was liable to induce the greatest consequences, hence it
was necessary to be very circumspect.
Here it was not possible to suspend the
law, as in England the Act of 1844 was
suspended, permitting an excess of the
official limit for the note issue, but the
banks could have been empowered to demand authority to change the proportion
enacted by the law creating National
Banks. They had no recourse to any of
these violations of the Statutes, which prove
only too often under such circumstances
that regulation by law is impossible; they
satisfied themselves, without having the
public powers intervene, with issuing
clearing-house certificates, that is to say,
promises, which they were bound to accept
as cheques in settling up the operations of
each day. It was through this help that
the Metropolitan Bank was enabled to resume payments on the 15th of May, the
evening of the day following its suspension. The Second National Bank was a

loser through the acts of its President, Mr. John C. Eno, but his father and the Directors hastened to make good the deficit. At this moment the excitement was intense, deposits were withdrawn, and 1 per cent. a day was paid, and even more, to obtain ready money or credit; under the influence of numerous sales of securities, exchange fell rapidly, metallic money was secured in London even, to be hurried to New York. Never could purchases be made under better auspices. Above all is this true when we observe that the condition of companies was much better known than in 1873.

The year 1883 had been disturbed by numerous failures. There had been no crash, but prices, far from advancing, had held their own with difficulty. On the eve of the breaking out of the panic there was complaint about the accumulation of goods in the warehouses, and of the difficulty of making exports. No scheme worked out, despite a very high protective tariff, and people were asking themselves what was its effect under the influence of unfavorable exchanges. Gold flowed away 'from the country, and cash on hand decreased each day.

On the 1st of January, 1884, the New York & New England Railroad was placed in the hands of a receiver by order of the court. The same thing happened on the 12th of January to the North River Company. In February, March, and April many houses exhibited their balance sheets. The fall in prices grew accentuated not only on the Stock Exchange, but in all markets. The discomfort increased until the 6th of May, the day on which occurred the failure of the National Marine Bank, whose President was associated with the house of Grant and Ward, which went down shortly afterwards with a liability of $17,000,000. This financial disaster made a great stir. Anxiety spread everywhere, when on the 13th of May the President of the Second National Bank of New York was also forced to suspend payment with a liability of $3,000,000; this was the final blow to credit. Every operation was suspended, all exchange became impossible; not securities but money was lacking. At one time the panic was such that the rate of discount and loans rose to 4 per cent. a day !

Although the panic was general, it was rather a panic of securities in the chief places of the United States, especially in New York.

One no longer knew on whom to count to provide ready money. Offerings were made on the Stock Exchange where there were no bidders, and the market disappeared in the midst of a panic which paralyzed every one.

This melancholy state of things was still further aggravated on the 14th of May by the failure of Donnel, Lawson, & Simpson and Hatch & Foote. On May 15th it was the turn of the Savings Banks of New York, of Fiske & Hatch, and of many others. It was impossible to obtain any credit from the banks, and all securities were unsalable, unless at ruinous rates. Reduced to such an extremity, it was necessary to adopt some course to help the market and avoid suspension of payments.

The certified checks issued by the banks did not answer, and it was necessary to

have recourse to a new means of settlement.
The members of the clearing house emerged
from their usual passive role to intervene
and to do a novel thing : they issued certificates that they accepted in the name of
the most embarrassed institutions whose
fall they wished to avert, in order to prevent the failure of others.   Then, as every-
body was making default, the Secretary of
the Treasury in his turn wished to aid the
common effort to sustain the credit of the
situation, and, in order to accomplish this
by the most regular methods, he pledged
himself to prepay the debt, whose term
was close at hand.

Despite these last helps it was easily seen
how great must be the disorder, to induce
recourse to such methods.   Never had they
been employed until now, which is proof
enough of the enormity of the situation,
whose equilibrium had been disturbed
since 1887, the year in which high prices
in everything had been reached on the
Stock Exchange.

To still further increase the joint respon-
sibility of the members of the clearing

house, it was agreed that a committee
should be charged with receiving as collateral bills and securities in exchange for
which certificates of deposit bearing 3 per
cent. were issued at the rate of 75 per cent.
of the amounts deposited. This agreement being adopted, a way to re-open the
National Metropolitan Bank was sought.
A selection made from its collection of
bills showed the securities it could pledge
for clearing-house certificates; and, its circulation being thus re-established, it was
enabled on May 15th to take part in settlements.

Upon the announcement of a syndicate
composed of the banks and the clearing
house, things settled down ; the general
distrust diminished ; there was the necessity
and wish to realize, but funds were lacking.

The rise in the discount rate attracted
foreign capital little by little, and exchange
grew easier. With the help of the syndicate the credit circulation became re-established, and the rate of discount declined to
5 per cent. For commercial needs money

was always to be had at 4½ per cent. and
at 5 per cent. when at the Stock Exchange
it was necessary to pay 4 per cent. per
day!

The panic was terrible from the 3d to
the 10th of May; for two days no one
wished to part with his money; it was impossible to borrow on any collateral, at
any price whatever. Hence came a decline
in the public securities, which fell below
the low prices of 1873.

The public complained that it could not
have foreseen the panic, because the loss of
gold had been concealed by the oft-repeated
assurance that there was a reserve of $600,-
000,000 in Washington.

Similar situations in 1857 and in 1873
were recalled, and it was remarked that
like troubles had not occurred until after a
long period of high prices, when capital
was scarce and the rate of interest high,
whereas this was far from being the case
at this period.

It was nevertheless notorious that the
decline in prices began two years back, that
the advance in prices had been stopped by

the breaking out of the panic of 1882 in
Europe, at Paris, and that since that
moment prices had begun to decline, less
rapidly, however, than in Europe, because
the shock had then merely disturbed a
market which had not yet recovered from
the panic of 1873, from which, in consequence of the Franco-Prussian war, France
had escaped. The mine not being suffi·
ciently charged in the United States the
explosion had not recurred. Speculation,
unable to restore a new impulse to the rise
in prices, was nevertheless able to hold its
own, until May, 1884, when the delayed
explosion finally occurred, covering the
market with ruins and bringing about a
liquidation with its accustomed train, a
great and lengthy decline of prices.

We may here note similar delays in the
breaking out of panics, in the period of
1837, 1839, 1864–1866 in France and in
England. Even an involved state of affairs
may be hidden by certain conditions, and
the situation, although itself exposed to the
same excessive speculation, may witness
the breaking out of the panic which has

been delayed for a certain time, only to occur simultaneously with the beginning of a decline of prices, and when it is thought that danger has been escaped.

As in Brussels and in the United States in 1837–1839 and in England in 1864–1866, large houses and powerful institutions of credit had maintained a whole scaffolding of speculation which was already out of plumb, but still able to stand upright through the general effect of the parts which connected them, and in this unstable equilibrium it sufficed for a single one to detach itself in order to overthrow the whole edifice at a juncture at which it was hoped it would continue to stand and even grow stronger. Does not this prove that after these epochs of expansion and activity characterizing prosperous periods (and there is no prosperous period without a rise in prices) a stoppage is necessary, a panic allowing a period of rest to permit the liquidation of transactions employed in helping to make a series of exchanges at high prices, and to allow the capital and savings of countries which had been too rapidly scattered and exhausted to reconstruct themselves during these years of tranquillity and of slackening business?

Confidence had already returned in New York despite the steady demands of the country bankers upon their correspondents, which pulled down the reserve below the legal limit; nevertheless in the midst of all the failures there was no suspension of specie payments.

The crisis of 1884, according to the Comptroller of the Currency, had been less foreseen than the crisis of 1873, and this notwithstanding it was sufficient to observe the number of enterprises and schemes flung as a prey to speculation, in order to foresee that financial troubles and disasters to the country must result.

The continuation of payments in gold, the low prices, and the outlook for a fine harvest gave courage, preserved the remaining confidence, and already allowed a speedy resumption of business to be anticipated.

The panic, although spreading over the whole Union, raged especially in New York.

8

Without wishing to expatiate upon its primary causes, the Comptroller of the Treasury could not help remarking that it had shown itself under the same circumstances as recently as in 1873; above all there were issues for new enterprises; the speculation had rushed to take them up at a premium, and people now asked their true value.

At this juncture railroad earnings, instead of increasing, showed weakness, and suffered a slight reaction; the solvency of houses interested began to be doubted; new loans were refused them, and immediately the artificially constructed edifice gave way.

To advance prices on the Stock Exchange, the banks had made immense loans on the shares and obligations of the new railway issues, and as soon as quotations, artificially maintained at the rates to which they had been carried, began to drop, everything became unsalable. Until this occurrence, led on and fascinated by the rise in prices, every one had bought; hardly was the advance arrested when every one reversed their operations at the same time. The bankers had loaned not only their capital but in addition a part of their clients' deposits ; brokers had encouraged a speculation which brought them business; and thus it was that all hands had flung themselves upon a path that could only lead to ruin.

The Comptroller of the Currency remarks with pride that, in the midst of the general upheaval and numerous failures of honorable houses, only two National Banks were involved : one of them failed, the other suspended payment.

The amount of liability of the banks and bankers of New York who succumbed during the month of May was estimated at $32,000,000, whereas that of the only National Bank which shared their fate did not exceed $4,000,000, the bank which suspended not having occasioned any loss.

Unhappily the year did not pass without its being necessary to mention new misfortunes : eleven National Banks failed, and it is a fact that among the banks and private bankers more than a hundred were counted in the list.

Despite the close watch bestowed upon the banks it was surprising to uncover all the tricks to which the National Marine Bank of New York was given over, and which until now had escaped the official examiners.

It suspended payment on May 6th, and the same day it was debited with $555,000; the books had been erased and overcharged for the benefit of one client alone to the amount of $766,000. He was a debtor to the amount of $2,400,000, six times the Bank's capital, and a portion of this debt was under a good many names of subordinate clerks. This same client had three open accounts, one as administrator, then a general account, and a special account. The whole thing was fictitious; the schemers sought to conceal irregularities, and had thus imposed on the examiners and on the Directors themselves.

The certificates issued by the clearing house, when credit had entirely disappeared, rendered a great service and sustained a great number of houses in equilibrium, which without this assistance must have succumbed. They were granted especially to the banks belonging to the Association, in order to make their daily settlements.

During the crisis of 1873 the same means had been resorted to, but too late; the panic was already at its height and the commotion general, so that nothing could re-establish confidence. This was not the case in 1884: the rapidity and decision with which the Associated Banks took steps gradually re-established confidence throughout the country. The maximum of issue did not exceed $24,900,000, of which $7,000,000 were for the National Metropolitan Bank; from the 10th of June balances at the clearing house were paid in legal money. Commercial paper, which for the most part was the collateral for these certificates, had already been redeemed. The Metropolitan National Bank alone requested time to liquidate.

The issue of these certificates was very rapid: $3,800,000 on the 15th day of May, $6,800,000 on the 16th, $6,700,000 on the 17th, or more than $17,000,000 in these first three days; then on the 19th, 20th, and 22d, $1,500,000, and that was all. The remainder of the amount was given in driblets. Payments, although slower, were made from the 1st of July to the 1st of August.

Let us now run over these occurrences: in 1873 instead of $24,900,000 in certificates $26,565,000 had been issued; $22,-000,000, had been issued between the 22d and the 29th of September, the redemptions took place from the 3d of November to the 31st of December.

In both cases the same amount, so to speak, had been sufficient to answer for all needs. If so small a difference sufficed to save a disordered market, people could not understand why panics could not be provided against. It was necessary to remember that this assistance was only felt when the decline of prices had already re-established an exchange of goods, bringing about the liquidation of houses unfortunately involved.

From the month of June, owing to the bank balances or the rate of exchange, the tranquillity and steadiness which had become re-established grew daily; after the storm of the first few days no new disasters had occurred except the failures of Mathew and of Morgan.

The position of the market grew firmer and the clearing house reduced its loan certificates, which now replaced the former excessive issues of bank notes. From $24,-000,000 they had already decreased to $18,000,000; of this amount $6,000,000 were taken by banks as a last resource, and there then remained only $12,000,000 in circulation. These $6,000,000 had served to sustain the shaken banks, and it is pleasant to state that outside of these requirements the amount needed was no larger.

Failures had ceased in the great centres, but they continued in the interior of the country ; the shock, like a great wave, took a certain time to overrun the various States.

Succession of Panics in the United States Studied through the Balances of the Banks. —Following the historical summary of panics in the United States it will be useful to have a general table, so as to glance at the very rare documents which permit us to follow the working of the Banks through their balance sheets. We know their organization, and we take upon ourselves to state results flowing from it.

It strikes us at once that abuses and panics have constantly occurred. Can we note a difference in the frequency and gravity of the casualties, according to whether we observe them working under the former or the new (the National Bank) system, inaugurated during the War of the Secession in 1864, when the machinery ' for the issue of bank notes was insufficient for the new requirements ?

Without lingering over the regulations before and after 1864, let us consider the differences we may ascertain by examining the balance sheets. Unfortunately, the exactness of our observation is lessened on account of the very diversity of the field it covers.

In the case of the banks of the United States we have had to content ourselves with the returns that the Comptroller of the Currency gives in his annual report on a stated day during the months of February, May, June, October, and December, beginning with the year 1865. Before that period we had only the yearly situation of the banks of the different States upon one given day; we are better informed on the second period; however, basing our conclusions upon the few balance sheets we possess, we ascertain the same series of development and increase. Although there are lapses, still, from another point of view, the table will be more complete, because it embraces all the banks of the United States. On such an extended field, it is true, we risk seeing great discrepancies disappear and lose themselves in the magnitude of the amounts whose movements we follow. In order better to grasp them, we have put before us the returns of the banks of the United States, together with those of the Associated Banks of New York City; we may thus recognize and follow the share played by each of them.

During the first period of the State Banks (1811–1864), the increase in the number of the banks was continuous, except for two stoppages, in 1841 and in 1862; in 1841, during the liquidation of the

panic of 1839, and in 1862 at the beginning of the War of Secession ; the crisis of
1857 did not interrupt the movement.

The capital of the banks had followed
the same changes. From $52,000,000 in
1811 to $358,000,000 in 1840, a reduction
to $196,000,000 in 1846, and finally the
last maximum reached in 1861, $429,000,-
000, at the breaking out of the war. In
1864 a new organization of the banks
under the name of "National Banks"
presented to the State Banks, without
suppressing them, a state of affairs destined to cause their liquidation, which, in
fact, practically occurred.

As in England and France, the amount
of discounts, as the balance sheets give it
to us, rose each year during the prosperous period.

Thus from 1830 to 1839 it reached
$492,000,000 from $200,000,000, to decline
again to $254,000,000 at the end of the
liquidation in 1843.

In the following period the same rising
movement from $254,000,000 to $344,000,-
000 was reproduced in 1848. The panic

in Europe burst forth in 1847; it re-
sounded very slightly in the United States
in 1848, as its subsequent liquidation in
1849 indicates, which only reduced the
local discounts to $332,000,000.

A new period of prosperity followed the
preceding events; the growing movement
re-appeared, and from $332,000,000 carried
the amount of the discounts to $684,000,-
000 between 1849 and 1857. The panic
broke out simultaneously throughout the
whole world; but notwithstanding the
wrecks it caused, such was the saving already, so healthy was the general situation
of business, that, after having thrown out
a little scum, the current of affairs resumed
its course until 1861, and discounts had already reached the amount of $696,000,000.
This amount is greater than that we have
noted in 1857, but at that time (whilst the
movement continued in Europe up to
1864), despite the shock it received by the
declaration of war here, there was complete stoppage until the end of the struggle; we have here come across a political
panic, not a business one. Peace re-estab-

lished, the movement resumed its course under new conditions and with a reorganization of the banks under the name of "National Banks." A change was due, but, as everything was made ready, it was speedy. The first balance sheet of the National Banks dates from 1864. The amount of discounts had already exceeded the sum of $100,000,000 in 1865, and grew to $500,000,000 in 1866. Once started the movement took its own course :

1865......$166,000,000	1870......$725,000,000
1866.......500,000,000	1871.......831,000,000
1867........609,000,000	1872.......885,000,000
1868.......657,000,000	1873.......944,000,000
1869.......686,000,000	

The yearly progression was interrupted as in Europe, and the explosion occurred at the same time. The rise in prices stopped, and incipient liquidation became apparent at the end of the year, and reduced the amount of paper on hand to $846,000,000, but, instead of lasting, as in Europe, a movement of revival, analogous to that which had followed the panic of 1864 in England, occurred. The amount of

discounts rose from $856,000,000 to $984,-
000,000 in 1875, and then, and then only,
the real retrograde movement showed itself
as in Europe, and reduced the amount of
the discounts to $814,000,000 in 1879,
simultaneously with the movement in
France and in England, when prices had
reached the lowest quotations, and when a
resumption of business was about to occur.
In a word, affairs resumed their course ;
from the end of the year the amount of
paper discounted rose to $933,000,000, and
the steady advance as set forth in table
No. 3 continued each year, until it reached
$1,300,000,000 in 1884. The panic had
burst forth in Europe in 1882, and the
agitation, so lively was its impulse, lasted
during eighteen months ; but, as we have
stated, the rise in prices ceased in 1882.

Starting from this time, a reaction appeared. The paper on hand lowered to
$1,200,000,000 in 1885. This liquidation
was scarcely noticeable, because we cover
the whole Union, and there is always an
upward movement in the new portions of
it which have not yet taken part in busi-

ness movements. If we note what occurred in the Associated Banks of New York, the very place where the greatest amount of business is carried on, the depression of the amount of paper on hand is most noticeable after the inflation observed at the height of the panic, while the decrease that we point out showed itself more slowly with the slackening of business. Thus, in the last period, the greatest amount of paper appears on hand—at the close of 1881, $350,000,000, and the minimum in December, 1884, the very year the panic had burst forth, and when, during the first months, the sum of $351,000,000 reappeared once more; except for a million, exactly the same amount there was in 1881.

This maximum amount was only an accident, under the influence of pressing needs at the time of the difficulty, for since 1881 the yearly reduction of the maximum and minimum amounts ensued. This tendency had occurred suddenly, and disappeared likewise; the resumption dating from 1885, a year sooner than in Europe.

The discounts of the New York Banks,

which had been reduced to $287,000,000, rose immediately upon the opening of the new period of prosperity, and a growing activity carried them to $408,000,000 in 1889 ; after a few more fortunate years we come to the end of the period of prosperity and high prices.

We gather the following about discounts from the balance sheets of the Associated Banks of New York. If we cast our eyes over the balance sheets of the National Banks of the Union, we must note a falling off of $100,000,000 in the paper discounted, that is, from $1,300,000,000 to $1,200,000,- 000 (1884–1885). After this short period of stoppage, clearly indicating the necessity for liquidation, discounts resumed their steady expansion, and rose to $1,470,000,- 000 in 1886, to $1,587,000,000 in 1887, and finally to $1,684,000,000 in 1888, when we were in the midst of a period of development and consequently of high prices and of prosperity ; and the same is true in France and England.

The study of a single section of the balance sheets, that of discounts and loans, has allowed us to follow the periods of prosperity, of panic, and of liquidation. When we next consider the other sections, we find the confirmation of our anticipations. Among these sections, in the order of importance, we notice first, public deposits in the form of running accounts; they constitute the reverse of the loans and discounts, whose total is immediately credited to the banks' clients, and the increase of paper on hand also follows. From 1865 to 1873 the steady increase was uninterrupted, viz., from $183,000,000 to $656,000,000 ; the maximum amount shows itself in the first quarter of 1873, eight months before the maximum of discounts and loans; in 1888 they ran down to $622,000,000 ; there is, say, a difference of $300,000,000 between the two totals, and this difference is the same, we observe, as that between the highest and the lowest of the two sections, as we notice it in the same year, during the liquidation of the panic of 1873.[1]

[1] See table of balance sheets of the Banks of the United States.

In the last period the progression is the same; from $598,000,000 the amount of deposits advanced to $1,350,000,000, whilst discounts and loans reached $1,684,000,000; that is to say, there was still a difference of $334,000,000. The relationship of the two sections was much more marked than in France and in England, where the amounts carried in accounts current vary more.

In the United States we then experienced a market based on credit, which, through discounts or loans by the banks, had reached the amount of the accounts current, and was about to call the clearing house into action to settle debts every-where.

The office of the circulation of bank notes, subsequent to the severe regulations enacted in 1863 for the organization of National Banks, had varied in the last two periods that we are studying. From 1863 to 1873, after the war troubles, in proportion as greenbacks were withdrawn, the bank notes issued by the National Banks not only took their place, but replaced

9

those of the State Banks, whose position the National Banks had taken.

We observe them rise firstly from $66,-000,000 to $341,000,000 (1865–1873) at the sharpest period of the panic. We might even charge them with causing it, if the disproportion alone of the two sums, $341,-000,000 bank notes compared with $944,-000,000 of bills discounted, did not at once repel this theory. It is only necessary to glance at this idea to see its falsity.

The maximum circulation of bank notes has here coincided with the panic, a thing which had not happened either in France or in England for a long time, and instead of presenting its highest figure during the liquidation of the panic of 1873, it shows us its lowest figure, $290,000,000 in 1877. Far indeed from increasing at this time as happened in Europe, the amount of bank notes in circulation decreased by means of the ebbs of metallic cash into the coffers of the banks : in reality the cause was lacking here; the ebb of specie was hardly felt at all.

With $4,000,000 in 1865, the reserve was poorly provided, increasing to $48,-

000,000 in 1870. At the end of the bursting forth of the panic of 1873 it became reduced to $10,000,000, at the worst of the panic to $16,000,000 ; then, under the influence of a slight whirl, it rose to $33,-000,000 in 1874, without reaching the highest figure of the preceding period, but soon the flow reappeared and reduced this metallic reserve to $8,000,000 in 1875. It was not until after this depression that the true ebb reappeared, when the circulation of bank notes was at its lowest figure ($290,000,000).

Whilst the $8,000,000 specie reserve grew successively to $54,000,000, $79,000,-000, $109,000,000, and finally to $128,000,-000 in 1878, 1879, 1880, and 1881 ; that is to say, upon the approach of the panic, the circulation also expanded from $290,000,-000 to its highest figure $323,000,000 in 1882, the year of the European crash and of the stoppage of the rise of prices in the United States. As to the minimum amount of the specie reserve, it is to be noted in 1883, between the critical years 1882 and 1884.

Metallic reserves are too small in the United States for their fluctuations to exhibit the same regular course they offer us in Europe; the least need exhausts them, and the smallest payments fill them to overflowing. The panic soon brought about a default in payment and a need of metallic money to re-establish equilibrium, but this remedy, if it does precede panics, sometimes precedes them by a year, as we have observed in 1883, and the same irregularity is apparent whether we observe the banks of the whole United States, or the Associated Banks of the City of New York.

After the panic of 1882–1884, the ebb of specie into the coffers of the National Banks of the United States and of the Associated Banks of New York resumed its usual course, and raised its level in the case of the National Banks from $97,000,-000' to $177,000,000 between 1883 and 1885, and even to $181,000,000 in 1888. This ebb occurred both in England and France at the same time, proving that cash reserves do not increase to the detriment of each other; it is a flood of specie or of bar-gold rendered easily available, through the conclusion of the decline of prices and the slackening of business, extending to the whole world, and in which each one partakes in proportion to its wealth, and above all in proportion to its credit circulation, and of the perfection of the settlements by means of clearing houses.

This regular course in the metallic reserves is no longer to be noted in the circulation of bank notes; instead of increasing and of entering its exchanges during the return of specie into the coffers of the banks, they again took part in the paper-money reserves. From $323,000,000 in 1882 we see the circulation of bank notes decrease each year little by little until it is reduced to $151,000,000 in 1888 ; and this remarkable fact confronts us in the face of an unheard of expansion of business, almost 50 per cent. greater than in 1873 ; and of a twofold simultaneous reappearance of $84,000,000 specie and of $172,000,000 bank notes. What then is the role of specie and of bank notes in the course of business in the United States ?

Much inferior to that which it plays in Europe in the absence of the machinery of a clearing house embracing the whole country, instead of being limited to some large cities.

The multiplicity of banks has strikingly helped the economic progress of the United States. From 1,500 National Banks in 1865 with a capital of $393,000,000, the number rapidly rose to 2,089 in 1876.

The panic of 1873 did not hinder the movement; however, during its liquidation, the number shrank to 2,048, only to rapidly advance to 2,500 by the close of 1882, and 2,664 in 1884, and this movement did not even suffer a slackening as in 1873 during the liquidation of its crisis; it continued steadily, and we enumerate 3,120 banks in 1888.

The increase is a third more than in 1876, but it is far from being thus in the case of the capital, which only rose from $504,000,000 to $588,000,000—that is, only 16 per cent. The small banks in the new centres of population are the factor, then, which annually increases the number.

The Condition of Business in 1888-92.[1]—
The year 1888 was fairly prosperous despite a Presidential election, but securities
were heavy, depression was general, and
some few stocks shrank amazingly. Excessive issue of new railroad securities and
disastrous competition between certain of
the Southwestern roads were without
prudence. Money was easy, bank-note
circulation continued to decrease till it was
only $151,000,000, and legal tenders to
$81,000,000, but specie reserve rose to
$181,000,000, the banking capital to $592,-
000,000 plus, the exports to $1,350,000,-
000, and discounts and loans rose to
$1,684,000,000.

The sharp speculations in wheat and the
formation of the French copper corner
caused a certain fluctuation in general business. Large crops, excepting wheat; a
flourishing cotton manufacture, a decline
in production of petroleum by agreement,
a 6 per cent. decline in pig-iron production,
a very heavy one in Bessemer iron, and a

---

[1] The facts I state in this *résumé* are based upon statistics
printed in the *Commercial and Financial Chronicle.*—DEC.
W. THOM.

very small export trade as compared with imports occurred. But in the year 1889, the export movement, consisting largely of cotton, was very great, being the greatest since 1880, and near the maximum, and compared favorably with the immense imports induced by the new tariff of 1890. In fact, the year 1889 surpassed all its predecessors in the volume of trade movements; the bank clearings showing an increase of 13 per cent. over 1888. The cotton, corn, and oats crops were the largest ever raised, and the wheat crop was almost the largest. But cotton brought fair prices, and cotton manufactures and production of iron were also considerably ahead of any previous year, while petroleum played an important part at good prices. Railroad earnings showed a wonderful recovery from 1888, and many reports gave the largest figures ever recorded.

During this year many consolidations and a number of foreclosures occurred. Railroad building fell to 5,000 miles compared to 7,000 in 1888. In general business, manufacturing and trade were extremely active, yielding plenty of work, good wages, and fair profits.

But the wool crop and its manufacture, a decline in the anthracite coal production, farm-mortgage pressure in the middle West, and low rates for corn and oats were untoward circumstances. Speculation on the general exchange was small, indicating a growing congestion, as was proved by the low bank reserves, especially in the last quarter of the year; but there was a heavy absorption of investment securities.

Gold, to the amount of $37,000,000, was exported in the first six months. A small amount of it returned before 1890.

Failures exceeded those of 1888 by 203 in number and about 20 per cent. in money. The woollen trade contributed much of this showing.

Importations surpassed all previous years, while exports exceeded them by nearly $20,000,000, and the net export of gold amounted to nearly $40,000,000. Money was easy during the first quarter, and then for a week a 10 per cent. rate occurred.

Thereafter, excepting the usual July 1st hardening, easy rates prevailed till August. Stiffening and fluctuating rates ensued till 30 to 40 per cent. in exceptional cases had been reached in December.

During the year, bank circulation declined to $126,000,000. Specie reserve sank to $164,000,000 and rose to $171,-000,000 with the ending of the year; legal tenders to $84,000,000, and the number of banks rose to 3,326; their capital to $617,000,000; their deposits to $1,436,-000,000, and their discounts and loans to $1,817,000,000, and surplus and undivided profits to $269,000,000.

Unused deposits, capital, surplus, and undivided profits were growing very small in comparison with loans and discounts at the end of the year.

The banks had to work closely, and the demands of the South and West for currency were severely felt.

Panic of 1890.—In this condition the year 1890 opened, and, with ever growing pressure for bank accommodation, displayed great activity throughout all departments of trade and transportation, with an un-equalled volume of transactions.

But it was as impossible to grant to the overtrading the money needed,—though the Secretary of the Treasury, in seventy days, threw a million a day into the market by buying Government Bonds,—as it had been for the "Gentleman's Agreement" of 1888 —that of the chief railroad presidents—to maintain rates, to permanently sustain prices of railroad securities against an over-supply of them; however, both delayed the inevitable.

The debates on the silver question in Congress, leading to hopes of cheap money, and the higher prices due to this temporary and delusive stimulus; the large gross railroad earnings, demand for structural iron; the Buenos Ayres crisis, leading London to ship us large amounts of our securities; our small wheat, oats, and corn crops, and large cotton crop; the tariff dis-cussion, ending with the McKinley Bill on October 6th, and the low bank reserves and money pressure beginning in August and lasting pretty steadily till December, and

an immense shrinking of securities, were
the chief features of the year ; and failures
beginning with that of Decker, Howell, &
Co., in New York, on November 11th, and
reaching a climax with the embarrassment
of Baring Brothers [1] in mid-November,
which failure itself greatly accelerated the
panic, were the chief events of the year.
Railroad building had increased to 6,081
miles, and the consequent new securities
were poorly absorbed.   Manufactures were
generally prosperous.

The huge imports to take advantage of

[1] Meanwhile Messrs. Charles M. Whitney & Co., David
Richmond, J. C. Walcott & Co., Mills, Roberson, & Smith,
Randall & Wierum, Gregory & Ballou, P. Gallaudet & Co., had
failed in New York, the North River Bank of that city had
been thrown into a receivership, and in Philadelphia the failure
of Messrs. Barker Brothers, had been followed by a number of
others.   This was all bad enough, but sinks into insignificance
when we recall the financial terror inspired by the great and
historic house of Baring Brothers proving unable to meet its
engagements, amounting to about £28,000,000.   The Bank of
England received notice of its difficulties on September 7th,
and by the 15th had secured from a syndicate, composed of the
great London houses, a guaranty that it would be protected
from loss to the amount of £4,000,000 if it would liquidate
the Barings' business, and from the British Government the
right to issue £7,000,000 of notes provided that sum was used
to loan the Barings, and it therefore assumed on that date the
task of paying the Barings' acceptances of £21,000,000 and

old tariff rates absorbed much money, while the Baring liquidation and that of other houses identified with South American enterprises, and the distrust bred by our Silver Bill caused a return of our securities, necessitating such a curtailment of credit that our panic took place. From July through December 31st, money ruled high and fluctuating.

The year shows a decline in circulation to $123,000,000, a decline of specie reserve to $178,000,000 with a subsequent rise to $190,000,000, a decline in legal tenders to $82,000,000, and of deposits to $1,485,-

---

£7,500,000 of other liabilities. Thus was averted what would probably have been the greatest panic in the world's history. That which occurred was a mere bagatelle to what was threatened. It is difficult to bestow too much credit upon Mr. William Lidderdale, Governor of the Bank of England, for conceiving and managing this plan. He has saved hundreds of thousands of homes and interests from misery. Under his able administration it is expected to extinguish the Barings' liabilities without calling on the Government, and it is believed something will be saved for the Barings from their former assets in business. This is deeply to be wished, for though the Barings have continued business under form of a stock concern with a million pounds capital, they are wonderfully restricted as compared with their former state. They have performed in banking too many helpful actions in furtherance of civilization to be eclipsed without sincere regret.

000,000, while the banks increased to 3,573 with a capital of $657,000,000, and a surplus and reserve of $316,000,000, and discounts and loans rose to $1,932,000,000.

The year 1891 has exhibited the usual incidents succeeding a time of reorganizations after panics and, after a period of selling and settlement, a rehabilitation of affairs and the consequent advance in prices of securities. The unprecedented abundance of our crops as a whole, coupled with the almost universal shortage in European countries, largely aided the rehabilitation. Bank balances reflected this startlingly. On February 26, 1891, loans and discounts and over-drafts amounted to $1,927,654,-559.80. On May 4, 1891, loans and discounts and over-drafts amounted to $1,969,-$46,379.67. On the former date capital, deposits, surplus, and undivided profits amounted to $2,462,456,677.92, and on the latter date to $2,567,288,143.45.

On July 9, 1891, discounts, loans, and over-drafts amounted to $1,963,704,948.07, and capital, deposits, surplus, and undivided profits to $2,522,609,679.78.

Confidence is restored and prices have advanced, and should advance still further. There seem to be only three things that could check the advancing market, and of those the two chief ones seem pretty surely relegated to a fairly distant future. These latter two are, in the order of importance: (1) a free silver law, *i.e.*, a law making, say, 67 cents' worth of silver pass for an equivalent of a 100-cent dollar; and (2) a very radical and abrupt change in our tariff law. The remaining and very minor influence is the breaking out of a general European war, which would at first induce a selling of our securities, and so lower prices, but which finally and shortly would benefit us by a subsequent returning flood of money exchanged for our various bread-stuffs, and supplies, and even securities of different sorts.

It would be better for our future if the liquidation of the last panic had been more radical in some cases, notably in land speculation. In this liquidation has not been thorough, and, as far as these cases influence the market, it has remained for a long time

unsound, and even now is not fully recovered.

The past twelve months have witnessed
a continued settling of old accounts, and
the undertaking of new business, in a limited
way, despite a somewhat uneasy feeling
about silver and the now accomplished
Presidential election. But the fact that an
analysis of the bank returns to the Comptroller of the Treasury shows that available
resources (capital, deposits, surplus, and
undivided profits), as compared with demands (loans and discounts), are good and
growing, considered in regard to the other
signs indicating prosperity (see Introduction), justifies the prediction of the steady
development of a prosperous period.

Panic of 1893-4.—It was early in 1893 that I wrote the last page of *A Brief History of Panics in the United States.* Two of the three checks to business prosperity to which I then referred, virtually occurred very soon. The determined resolve of the "free silver" members of Congress to continue the heavy monthly utterance of silver dollars redeemable at par in gold kept many business men most disquieted. They saw that the free gold in the Treasury was sinking greatly and steadily. They knew, also, that there was semi-official assertion of the right of the United States to redeem its silver dollars in Government notes. The Free-Coinage Bill had been passed by the Senate in July. The House defeated it. The legal fights against certain great railroad combinations and frequent labor strikes put additional burdens on the market.

In the United States and abroad the doubt of our willingness and ability to redeem our obligations at par in gold on demand grew most rapidly. Accordingly,

10

exports of gold increased and hoarding of it began at home. To all this was added the expectation of a severe downward revision of our tariff laws if the Democratic Party should succeed, as was expected, in the Presidential election in November.

Business was scared and slowing down and, therefore, using less and less of its working capital. The false ease of increasing loanable funds in the custody of the banks lulled many into a specious confidence. But gold was exported in increasing quantities. Should the Government issue bonds in exchange for gold for the purposes of redemption? The Philadelphia & Reading receivership occurred. Easy money led to many consolidations of transportation properties and to very many large commitments. Money tightened. In March, it loaned at 60% per annum. Would President Cleveland call an extra session of Congress in March to repeal the silver law and to issue bonds in order to replenish the free gold in the Treasury? The

Stock Market showed a great decline in quotations.

In April, 1894, Secretary of the Treasury Jno. G. Carlisle forbade the further issuance of gold certificates for gold deposited in the Treasury under Act of July 12, 1882, whenever the gold in the Treasury "reserved for the redemption of United States notes falls below $100,000,000." This further alarmed the business world, which was not reassured when on the 20th Carlisle announced that the Treasury would pay gold for all Treasury notes so long as he had "gold lawfully available for that purpose." President Cleveland, that stalwart man, uttered this high and firm pronouncement on April 24th: "The President and his Cabinet are absolutely harmonious in the determination to exercise every power conferred upon them to maintain the public credit, to keep the public faith, and to preserve the parity between gold and silver and between all financial obligations of the Government." Very good, thought business, but how and when will you act accordingly?

Lack of business confidence increased greatly. Money rates advanced. Security values fell; imports greatly exceeded exports. Silver certificates were at 83. Something was about to snap in the general business machine. National Cordage broke from 57 to 15½ on May 1st, receivers were appointed, and the panic of 1894 had declared itself and grew worse on the 4th and 5th. Call money rose to 40%. June witnessed great distress in business circles. On the 27th the Government of India stopped the coinage of silver for individuals and decreed the exchange value of the rupee at 16 pence. This lowered the exchange value of our silver bullion certificates to 62. President Cleveland helped matters somewhat by announcing that Congress would be convened early in September. In early July the panic increased somewhat despite the President's call for Congress to assemble on August 7th. Time loans were hardly obtainable. Conditions in August grew worse. Business was almost at a standstill, and failures were very frequent. From August 7th until the affirmative action on the 28th by the House of Representatives as to the repeal of the Silver Act, there was great concern.

Then hope revived; but hoarding of currency increased. Great banking interests in New York helped the situation mightily by importing over $40,000,000 gold. September was an anxious but more hopeful month as the prompt adoption by the Senate of the Free-Silver Bill was anticipated. However, the weary debate dragged on in the Senate. President Cleveland demanded the unconditional adoption of the House measure. Certain compromisers, led by Senator Arthur P. Gorman of Maryland, suggested that during each of the following fifteen months the Government purchase the minimum amount of 1,000,000 ounces of silver, and then stop all such purchases against which silver certificates had to be issued. This plan for speedy action President Cleveland and the Secretary of the Treasury opposed as worthless unless concurrently there was an issue of $100,000,000 of Government bonds to replenish the gold in the Treasury. They asserted that new legislation must be had before any such bonds could be validated. So the business world continued to suffer.

Let me here state the fact, that without any fresh authorization, Secretary of the Treasury Carlisle did in January, 1895, issue $50,000,000 of Government bonds to replenish the free gold in the Treasury, and that an injunction suit against their sale was dissolved by Judge Cox at Washington on the 30th of that month. Gorman had been right. The credit of the country would not have suffered by the additional issuance of some final $60,000,000 (?) of silver certificates if the gold in the Treasury had concurrently been upbuilt to the extent of $50,000,000 to $100,000,000; but an immensity of business loss would have been averted.

But to resume the orderly recital of those times. October dragged along its weary length, while the Senate debated and business withered. Finally, on the

30th, the Senate accepted unconditional repeal of the Free-Silver Act. On November 1st, it became a law. The fear of repudiation thus escaped, though with fearful loss, the country plunged into all the unsettlement caused by a too sudden and too extensive change in the tariff. These changes were announced by the House Committee on December 27th.

The conditions mentioned in the last paragraph beginning on page 22 of the introduction to this book, were at work. Before the market had recovered from the "Silver panic" of 1893-4, the terror caused to the business world by the proposed very decided changes in the customs dues laid hold upon every trader in the United States and reflectedly upon every one of its citizens. It shook business throughout. Would not such a plan as is set forth in the footnote below[1]

[1] "Mr. DeCourcy W. Thom expressed himself yesterday as heartily indorsing the Democratic celebration to be held in this city January 17 next, to which all the party leaders will be invited and at which subjects of interest to the party will be discussed.

have virtually prevented all that?   When
I sent that plan, which I had stated in an
interview in the *Baltimore Sun* of December 24, 1910, to the various members of
the Finance Committee of the United

"When asked to give his opinion on some of the questions
worthy of discussion at this gathering Mr. Thom mentioned
the tariff and economy in the conduct of national affairs.

"In the coming national Democratic celebration," he said,
"I hope suggestions dealing with a rational reformation of
the tariff and the need for national economy of every kind
will be duly considered, and that on these two subjects alone,
to be treated thoroughly but temperately, will this national
Democratic gathering advise our party as to its best course to
pursue.

"In three successive Presidential canvasses since the Civil
War the Democratic party has received a majority vote of the
people of the United States, and in my opinion would have
gained three thereby, instead of the alternate two, elections to
the Presidency if the tariff issue, the major one of the two
great issues—namely, tariff and economy—on which they won,
had been so sought to be applied as not to threaten unduly to
affect general business."

PROTESTS AGAINST EXTRAVAGANCE

"All will agree with me that a reasonable economy, instead of the actual wild extravagance of government, is more
than ever a national need.   Who will disagree with me, that
in addition to the contribution from internal revenue, the
tariff should be used merely to contribute towards the due
expenses of the Government economically administered, but
so applied as not to break down the standard of American
citizenship, as exemplified in the working people of our

States Senate and to the Committee on Ways and Means of the House of Representatives, very many of them wrote me affirmatively on the subject.

To revert, however to the due order

country; and eked out, if it is possible, by contributions into the national treasury of sound inheritance taxes?"

URGES CUT ON NECESSARIES

" Is it not possible to apply that general plan as follows : Divide, say, all of the articles now upon the tariff list into three classes.

" (*a*) All such as are usually found in the typical American homes—I mean the homes of those admirably called by Grover Cleveland the 'plain people,' who are just the same class, I believe, as those indicated by Abraham Lincoln, when he said, 'God must greatly love the common people, for he made so many of them '—and put that list of articles on a free list or a severely tariff-for-revenue-only list.

" (*b*) Create a second division composed of all the articles of luxury. Put upon them the very highest tariff they will stand and yet come into the country, except in the case of articles of antique art. These latter should be admitted free.

" (*c*) Keep upon all other articles now in the tariff list the actual duties for the period of one year, but after that period and the actual imposition of the proposed new tariff I am discussing shall have begun, put all the articles involved in Class *c* upon a tariff-for-revenue-only basis, so constructed as not to break down the standard of the American workingman's living."

YEAR TO MARKET STOCK

" This period of one year—say, would allow manufacturers to market their stock on hand or already required to be pro-

of our tale. It was on January 17,
1895, that Secretary of the Treasury
John G. Carlisle, without any new legislative authority, offered to sell $50,000,000
Government bonds already mentioned.

---

duced on the basis of the market influenced by the quasi-
Government protection extended by the existing tax laws of
the nation.

"At the end of this period the manufacturer would be
obliged to produce at less cost in order to find a market in
competition with his foreign competitor, which competition
would result in lower prices that he and his foreign competitors
would have to offer to the working people and other citizens
of our country."

EFFECT ON WAGES

"Those working people and other citizens would for a year
have been enjoying at lesser cost all of the articles used in
the typical American home I have referred to and could without loss therefore well afford to submit to a reduction in wages
so long as that reduction in wages was contemporaneous with
affording them a proportionate or more than proportionate
reduction in cost of the articles for whose purchase those
wages were sought to be expended. At the same time, the
manufacturer at a proportionately lesser cost of production,
through this reduction in wage-paying, would be selling as
much or more of his old products at their old profit.

"Could we add to the income from the tariff and internal
revenue the sums derived from the sound national inheritance
tax I have mentioned above it is evident we would have sup-
plied for the period of change from one tax system to another
an 'adequate governor' to use a mechanical illustration, to
prevent undue oscillation of prices in the business world."

If issued during the Silver-repeal fight
when Gorman proposed his compromise,
and if Carlisle had made it clear very
early that as many such issues for gold
would be made as were needed to keep
the trading public safeguarded against
any monetary-business cramping caused
by the governmental policy affecting the
tariff, a minimum rather than something
approaching a maximum of disturbance
would have followed. In better spirits
because of the issuance of the $50,000,000
Government bonds for gold, the business

BANK RESOURCES TO PREVENT STRAIN

" The further use of the existing financial agencies for co-
operation of the banks in all sections to mass resources and
apply them to prevent undue local strain upon credit dispels
the fear of any necessary injury to the financial fabric in
effecting this change.

" Grover Cleveland, whose character and principles I have
long revered, seemed to me in the application of his plan for
tariff reform to have endangered at once the success and the
permanence of his reform of the tariff—which you recall was
confessedly and very properly not a reformation to free trade—
by failing to provide in it a method for avoiding or at least
minimizing and shortening any incident disturbance to the
business world. His plans, further, failed by not reasonably
insuring for the transition period from the old tariff to the
new one sufficient national income for national expenses."

world worked along. The House had passed the Tariff Bill early in February by a big majority. Business soon looked up decidedly. But the Seigniorage Bill was adopted in March. President Cleveland, that sturdy upholder of the Nation's credit, vetoed it. He knew that any new moral obligation to keep at a parity with gold dollars worth in themselves less than one hundred cents in gold would materially shake domestic and foreign credit.

The veto had a deservedly splendid effect upon all our trading interests. This was increased by the failure of the House to override the President's veto of the Seigniorage Bill. But the Senate had not acted on the Tariff Bill. Business dwindled and there occurred strikes and other widespread labor troubles, especially in the bituminous coal trade. In many parts of the country the militia, and in Chicago United States troops, had to be employed to maintain order. Call money was a drug on the market. The net gold in the Treasury was very low.

The Tariff Bill dragged its weary length along. President Cleveland and Chairman William L. Wilson of the Ways and Means Committee of the House insisted that the bill would produce sufficient revenue for the expenses of the Government. Senator Gorman and others in the United States Senate insisted to the contrary and demanded that the tariff on sugar should be kept at a high figure. A bitter controversy ensued. Finally, on August 13th, the House accepted the Senate Tariff Bill. It was time for some affirmative action, for among other threatening conditions the net gold in the Treasury had fallen to the lowest figure since resumption of specie payments in 1879.

Business began to revive. The issue of $50,000,000 Government bonds for gold to replenish the Treasury stock was a very stimulating influence. The improvement dated virtually from the agreement in February between the Government and the Morgan-Belmont Syndicate to prevent the export of gold. In June,

1895, the Government gold was thus brought up to a round $100,000,000 for the first time since December, 1894. But notwithstanding the fact that the business outlook was decidedly better, the inevitable disturbances to business following a general change in the tariff, unsettled political conditions in Europe and the selling of American securities owned abroad, the shortage of the American cotton crop, President Cleveland's Venezuela message, which many persons thought might bring on war with England, and another decline in the Treasury free gold, again shook business confidence.

Improvement, however, was stimulated by a remarkable increase in the supply of money in our balance of trade and by the virtual settlement of the Venezuelan question. The business situation was steadily clearing. The ills from the panic of 1893–4 were well behind us. The Spanish-American war proved to be harmless to us financially, while it tended to show that National neighborliness could be exercised in a splendidly unselfish way. By our treaty of peace with Spain on December 10, 1898, an additional emphasis was given to the revival of trade. During 1899 a great rush to speculate brought the pinches in money inevitable in those pre-Reserve Bank days, but could not stop the general broadening of business interests although the industrial situation was unsatisfactory in spots. Indeed, the succeeding year was to witness severe industrial trouble destined to cause a general setback in business. The situation cleared considerably when the November elections of 1900 showed the country to be safe from the Bryan silver policy.

Big business interests took hold of market conditions. Huge combinations of trade interests became the order of the day. The United States Steel trust was the vastest and was the transcendent achievement of J. Pierpont Morgan. The Stock Exchange was wild with speculation. The collapse came there in the famous decline of the 9th of May, 1901, precipitated by the Northern Pacific corner. In a month the market was tranquil again. The shooting of President McKinley produced great financial nervousness. The over-trading abroad, especially in Germany, was influencing us and all the rest of the world, which had not yet recovered from the vast financial cost of the English Boer War.

The ever increasing closeness of business relations the world over — their virtual solidarity, in fact—was being illustrated again with us. A chief example was trouble in the copper groups following a slackened world demand for their products.

Overtrading was doing its usual work. This induced loss of business courage in many quarters, or shall I say a realization that nowhere in the American business system was there any arrangement empowered so to marshal the competent strength of financial America that large and overwhelming disturbances should become impossible in business generally. Indeed, the Government forces seemed to tend contrariwise to big business practices. They took virtually their first step in "trust-busting" when they tried to break up the Northern Securities Company, which had been concocted to handle the celebrated Northern Pacific case. Labor troubles supervened. Many great speculative stock campaigns collapsed. The banks yielded to the imperative need to reduce credits. The year 1902 had almost experienced a widespread panic: but the marshaling of great private resources had restored confidence temporarily, and it closed in peace.

Panic of 1903.—Then came the real beginning of the protracted "trust busting" campaign. Business took fright, for it believed it was to be bullied rather than soundly regulated. Great failures on the Stock Exchange were its sure indications. Fear and distrust was upon all the American business world. Industries languished. Money was easy because less and less employed in trade. The great captains of industrial finance, however, patched up troubles and differ-

11

ences here and there and, availing themselves of the plentiful supply of money, soon had a notable speculation at work. Gradually the country took heart again and business experienced a revival.

It was thought that President Roosevelt, elected in November, 1904, would help bring about discrimination between "good" trusts and "bad" trusts, and whose "trust" is bad! But "trust busting" became an even more popular and political pursuit. Indeed, the abuses practised by many of them had created a situation regarding which the question was becoming in the popular mind simply this, "Shall trustdom rule the people or the people rule the trusts?" The sound control of both before the Constitution of their country must be the happy solution.

The Bill of May 9th of the House of Representatives, giving the Interstate Commerce Commission power to fix railroad rates, was ominous, and little noticed by the general business world; but some noticed and acted. The Senate

had not voted; nor did they realize what
rate-regulation implied to railroad balance
sheets and so to the Stock Exchange.
Some interest was selling securities. The
business public was awakening to the
fact that legislators, legislation, the people,
and the law were hot after the business
methods of many organizers. Fear,
founded on a tardy awakening to facts,
declared itself, but spasmodically, for
now and again the great captains of
finance and industry were trying to save
the situation. They successfully aided
whatever of momentum there was in
general business. But Congressional activity as to any combinations in restraint
of trade was unabated. It called upon
the President for such information as the
Interstate Commerce Commission might
have as to a combination in restraint of
trade between the Pennsylvania Railroad
and certain lines allied with it.

The battle between the old style and
the new style of managing great corporations was fairly on. Labor troubles
added to the existing disarrangement of

business. San Francisco's vast earth-
quake and consuming fire sucked much
capital away from financial centres in
order to replace the $350,000,000 of
capital destroyed. The money market
was greatly restricted. The stock market showed signs of panic. The Secretary
of the Treasury continued to help the
situation as best he knew how. Notably,
he offered $30,000,000 Panama Canal
Bonds, and very successfully sold them.
That afforded an additional basis for
bank-note issuing. The stock market
responded with a fine upward swing.
Heavy dividends were declared by certain
leading railroad and other corporations.
Indeed many high records were made by
securities and so distracted attention
from that steady tide of keener inspection
and stricter regulation by the agents of
the people which was destined to unmoor
and toss and injure many a financial
craft. Railroads asserted that the country needed a great increase in railroad
trackage, but that the actual treatment
of the roads deterred extensions through

frightening capital. So the year 1906 wore away after having sorely tried the nerves of the whole business world which it left in a most justly apprehensive state.

The Panic of 1907.—The panic of 1907 opened with great but feverish activity in business. Driven by necessity the railroads adopted the issuance of short-time notes for new capital, as the market would absorb no long-time obligations except at forbidding interest rates. Any signally untoward happening could promptly precipitate a **panic.** The United States Treasury withdrawal of Government deposits from the banks, and the collapse of the Knickerbocker Trust Company in New York were such happenings.

On March 14th, the panic declared itself and pandemonium ruled on the New York Stock Exchange,—that prominent barometer of business conditions. In its coming it had exemplified again the characteristic symptoms of a panic which I have set forth on pages 7–16 of the introduction to this book. After the spasm of March 14th and the business cataclysm of the following October, the business world staggered along, but with the strength merely that results from courage and the exercise of reserve power husbanding its resources and lightening its load. The decrescendo movement of another business cycle had begun. Runs on financial institutions were prominent in our country. But throughout all the western world resources were strained. Money had been overused. Money rates were extremely high. Failures were frequent everywhere. In our own country painful disturbances, relaxation, and unrest were everywhere apparent. The radical doctrines of many political leaders tended to further unrest.

The business of the country was halting between the need sanely to regulate "big business" and the fact that "big business" had been obliged to fight for prosperity in the welter of unallowable but very often undeniable conditions. The railroads justly claimed that they were forbidden living rates. Their opponents accused them of carelessness and waste. The railroads and the Interstate Commerce Commission were the protagonists respectively of the conservative and the radical thought of the country, which is so rich in natural wealth and is inhabited by so resourceful a people that though by statutes they be well managed or not, their National wealth increases. So ran the business world away, but with a very slow and steady approach towards a rational rectification of disputed legislation as affecting business. Meanwhile the courageous "captains of industry" were leading in business as best they could and were better appreciating the temper and needs of the American people.

Added to the difficulties resulting from our languishing trade at home, we suffered reflectedly from the constriction of business in Europe, which was acutely aware that the disturbance in the Balkans threatened to destroy the peace of Europe. Conditions were not yet quite ready there for a cataclysmic war. For example, statistics had not quite demonstrated to Germany that the physique of her people and the rate of increase of their families were declining while the expenditures for superpreparedness for war was demanding either retroaction in that regard or else an expenditure from the principal of their property. Germany did make in one year the sacrifice of five per cent. of her principal for yet fuller preparedness for war. Indeed since late in 1908, it is fair to say that consciously or unconsciously the whole world has been in travail. Whatever broad measures statesmen anywhere have promulgated, have been subjected to the unusual stress and strain of world-wide unrest. Like the treacherous undertow that wrenches those who venture in, has been the world unrest upon all phases, incidences, and predicates of business. Some of us have long realized this; some have not.

With November, 1908, came the election of that great constitutionist, Taft, to the American Presidency upon a platform less radical than that of his opponent. This heartened the constructive forces of the country. But very little upbuilding resulted. The coming revision of the tariff was of itself sufficient further to restrict business undertakings, and to cause many great producers of goods to arrange to unload at lowering prices their actual and their future outputs. But the conserving of resources since the panic had helped the superficial situation, and the spasmodic stimulus that so often follows a general heightening of the tariff showed itself after the adoption of the tariff bill in August, 1909.

The illness and after a month or two the death of the great business leader, Harriman, caused in the securities market a great decline. Fundamental conditions were unsettled. The best that could be expected was a see-saw movement until some power should set our country and the business world at large once more securely on their respective bases. The Anti-Trust Law, the Interstate Commerce Law, and such like influences continued to disturb the United States, while Europe was beneath the surface unendingly agitated.

General business marked time while statesmen or pseudo-statesmen planned and promised panaceas. President Taft joined that populous group. The securities market, that barometer of business, fell beneath such assurance of further unsettlement. How can you continue to trade unless reasonably sure that conditions will remain fairly constant! All this militated against a normally quick recovery from a great panic. Little scares were frequently experienced. Influences matured and presented one great political party split into two great factions, while the other chief party endured something of the same development.

A conservative handling of National policies, or a radical one was the question in each case. The November elections indicated a popular revolt against the party in power—the Republican. Unshaken, President Taft followed his convictions and in his Presidential message, of December, 1910, to Congress called for a halt in legislating to regulate corporations, until the effect of the laws on the statute books could be studied. The stock, money, and industrial markets were marking time. Not to go forward in business or elsewhere is in itself to retrograde. Thus opened the year 1911. Under the influence of easy money, better business on some of the western railroads, better dividend declarations here and there, a rosy prediction as to the early future of the iron market, and the belief that the Interstate Commerce Commission would grant better rates to the railroads, general business felt encouraged and prices advanced somewhat. But in February the Interstate Commerce Commission forbade the railroads any increase whatever in rates. The roads were obliged to institute many cramping economies which to them very often meant the using up of their corpus and to the business world of the United States a permeating retrogressive influ-

ence.   Reductions in railroad dividends
were symptomatic of that.   To add to
all this there developed additional business unrest predicated in the general tariff
change favored by the House of Representatives in April.

The United States Supreme Court
decision interpreting the Sherman Anti-
Trust Law of 1890 as affecting the
Standard Oil Company case and the
American Tobacco Company case were
delivered late in May and were unexpect-
edly reassuring to business.   This was
another evidence that the best thought
of the Nation everywhere was seeking
to rectify the looseness of the past without
killing business initiative and continued
endeavor.   So matters see-sawed in the
business world.   It was indeed in a state
of unstable equilibrum.   Stocks declined
now abruptly; then, after some slight
recovery, gently; but the slant was
decidedly downward.

The Government felt that its duty
required it to push forward the investiga-
tion of industrial corporations; and that

the Nation so demanded. And it was in October that the chief of such corporations—the United States Steel Trust— had a Government suit for dissolution filed against it. The sturdy bell-wether of the corporation flock was attacked by the great United States Government. What would happen to the humbler members of the flock! Certain court decisions were reassuring to corporations in November and business brightened for the time being and during much of December in certain notable instances, for in that month the Interstate Commerce Commission report appeared and seemed less drastic in tone.

The year 1912 opened with an additional influence promising increased alarm and marking of time. I mean that candidates for the Presidential nomination began their canvasses, which, of course, implied new plans for making new laws to govern business conditions. Former President Roosevelt announced his candidacy in February. President Taft was already constructively in the field.

Governor Harmon of Ohio was mentioned in many quarters as a successful reformer who wished soundly to guide but not unwittingly injure business, while Underwood was similarly praised in addition to his record on the recasting of the tariff into a further revenue measure. Champ Clark, Speaker of the House of Representatives, was a popular candidate. And Woodrow Wilson loomed up as though forecast by destiny. At first and in many important sections of the country considerably more delegates to the Republican National Presidential Convention were chosen for Mr. Taft than for Mr. Roosevelt. This and brisker business served to hearten conservative interests, and the general market revived despite the decidedly downward influence in our country of the gigantic strike among English coal operators, who thereby spread trouble throughout the British Empire, and, through the solidarity of the financial world to-day, affected every financial centre.

The remainder of the year was dominated by the Presidential canvass.   Taft, called by many a "stand-patter"; Roosevelt, "the insurgent," who proposed to mend all the troubles of the political public by his usual brusque methods; and Woodrow Wilson, the "conservative with a move on," made their appeals for popular support.   Until the verdict in November a see-saw market took place in the United States, while Europe and reflectedly the remainder of the world became alarmed lest the war declared in October by the Balkan States against Turkey should produce world-wide trouble.

The November Presidential election showed that Woodrow Wilson received 435 votes, Mr. Roosevelt 90, and Mr. Taft 8.   However, the popular vote for Woodrow Wilson was more than 1,000,000 below that cast for Messrs. Roosevelt and Taft jointly, and about 2,000,000 short of a majority of all the votes cast for the Presidential nominees—Socialist, Republican, Democratic, and so on.   But the vitally significant fact is that the popular vote for the "stand-pat" candidate—

Mr. Taft—was very small in comparison with the joint vote of the three candidates whose platforms called for a drastic handling of National policies,—Debs, Roosevelt, and Wilson.

Drastic recasting of the rules of any game unsettles play. The market dropped. But fortunately for the country the ripe and balanced and active intellect and character of Woodrow Wilson, elected President, lent much re-assurance against the extensive political surgery he had been chosen to perform. All knew that he would be thorough and reasoning. All the grievous handicaps that business suffers from uncertainty of regulation, it was thought would be overcome as promptly as possible. But the pledged great change of the tariff was enough to induce retrenchment of business endeavor. With a major factor unusual in any proposition, how can stability, much less progress, be expected in any interest?

The Panic of 1913.—Retrogression in business began very early in 1913 and increased until mid-October, 1914. On October 3, 1913, the new Tariff had become a law; but other reforms still jostled business. However, by mid-October, 1914, the Interstate Commerce Commission seemed to have become less radical in its views, the Industrial Trade Commission was at work apparently studying the essentials of the industrial situation, the United States Supreme Court was delivering opinions in check of indeterminate statutory meddling with business and the splendid potential of the Reserve Bank system was offering for use.

It is hard not to overstate the vast re-assurance offered to business by linking together the banking power of the country through the Reserve Bank system. Just as an enormously large number of troops skilfully thrown into an endangered—a panicky—position will ensure success, so can the vast resources of the Reserve Bank system restore financial order when panic fear is declaring itself. During the past two years of threatening from

12

the disturbances in Mexico, our country
has learned to forecast the benefit that
the Reserve Bank system predicates;
but our stay and confidence has been the
cool and far-seeing statesmanship of our
great President, Woodrow Wilson.

The breaking out of the "World War"
in August, 1914, had so flooded our market
with securities held in Europe that the
Stock Exchange, following the conti-
nental example, closed from July 31st
till November 28th, when the New York
Stock Exchange and other American
stock exchanges opened for restricted
business in bonds and on December 15th
to unlimited trading in stocks and bonds.
Other kinds of exchanges acted much the
same. This checked business in every
direction, despite the great issuance of
temporary Clearing House certificates.
In two months the latter tendency was
changed in many quarters.

Then began the "war boom." Gradually it has spread, bringing such enormous
profits in all our lines of business supply-
ing the needs of the "Great War," that

the first twelve months of it showed more
than a billion dollars trade balance in our
favor, and that balance then began
increasing on a progressive scale. Money
is yet plentiful. All business is stimulated. Our crops are unexampled in
quantity and money value. Everything
points to great prosperity unchecked
until the "Great War" ceases and with-
draws the stimulating demand for our
supplies.

Then will come a readjustment of our
trade. Money will have become actually
or potentially scarce because of the
previous vast expansion of our business,
and all the banking power of our country
will be requisite to prevent a crashing
panic. The Reserve Banks will have
gotten fully to work by then, it is to be
hoped. They will be needed to lead in the
life-saving operations. Such first aid to
the injured will obviate such financial
sufferings as the old-time panics presented. They can hardly be expected
to reduce the casualties to the volume
of the slow panic in securities in the

year 1913, for the volume of business
involved at present is vastly more swollen
and the kind more circumscribed.

It is interesting to note that panics
have continued to appear about as regularly as usual, but less crushingly, since
1890, the date up to which the first and
second editions of this book had traced
them. Remedial or partially preventive
measures have been more and more
utilized by the financial powers to control
them. Never will panics cease so long
as trade and fear are exemplified on this
earth, but just as modern medicine is
overcoming the dangers threatening the
physical man, so is modern finance
overcoming panic and the other dangers
which threaten financial stability. After
all, reserve power and only a rational use
of financial resources are the surest
preventive of panic. And that the American people have not been forced through
entrance into the "World War" to deplete
their reserve strength, especially in a
financial way, is due to the splendid
conduct of our great President. He is

leading this country to unexampled prosperity. Instead of consenting that old
abuses in the business world should
continue until an over-indignant public
had grown riotously injurious, he has
guided the current of their wrath, initiated
or promulgated the methods for redress-
ing their grievances, and has saved to the
country, to its people, and to general
business itself, the splendid and full
service of business enterprise freed from
the abuses and handicaps that unregu-
lated conditions had forced it to employ
in the unrestrained struggles of the open
mart.

DeCourcy W. Thom.

INDEX

Adams, President, 63
Agriculturists, how affected by protective tariffs, 5, 6, 11;
    how affected by low tariffs, 10, 12
Alabama indemnity, 99
American Tobacco Co. case, effect of decision on, 172

Balkan States trouble, causes alarm, 167, 175
Baltimore Sun, December 24, 1910, interview with Mr.
    Thom on the tariff, 151 *seq.*
Bank of England, extends help to America, in 1839, 73;
    suspension of, in 1796, 88; averts panic in 1890, 140
Bank of France, suspension of, in 1848, and 1871, 89
Bank of Lancaster, 29, 30
Bank of New York, surplus of, 57
Bank of North America, formation of, 26; embarrassment
    of, 27
Bank of Pennsylvania, charter obtained, 61
Bank of Philadelphia, 33
Bank of the United States, formation of, 28; reduces dis-
    counts and circulation, 36; re-establishment of, 39; terms
    and conditions of charter of, 40 *seq.*; examination of, by
    Congressional Committee, 49; violation of charter of, 49;
    insolvency of, 59; withdrawal of Government deposits
    from, 60; action of, in panic of 1838–39, 67; aids South-
    ern banks, 70; liquidation of, in 1839, 75; renewal of
    struggle with United States Government, 77; endeavor
    to force Government into bankruptcy, 77, 78; opinion
    of Buchanan concerning, 79
Bankruptcies, in England in 1839, 75, 76
Bankruptcy, endeavor of United States Bank to force the
    Government into, 77, 78
Banks, advances beyond resources as cause of panic, 36;
    new, 1811–1815, 36–37; embarrassment of local, 1828–
    29, 54
Baring Brothers, failure of, 5, 140, 141
Barker Brothers, failure of, 140
Biddle, Mr., President of the U. S. Stock Bank, on crisis
    of 1825 in England, 54; obtains charter of Bank of
    Pennsylvania, 61; on action of Bank of U. S., 67, 68;

183

Printed in the United States
126703LV00001B/42/A